AF263639

Walter Carter

WW1 SOLDIER'S TALE

PART ONE
MARCH 1914 – JUNE 1915

LIVING HISTORY

Published by Living History
Home Farm
Ardington
Oxfordshire
OX12 8PN
info@livinghistorynow.co.uk

Copyright © Living History 2015

A catalogue record for this book
is available from the British Library

ISBN: 978-0-9935360-0-7

*While the events described in this book are based on fact, the characters are fictional
and any resemblance to real persons, living or dead, is unintended.*

CONTENTS

List of Characters

<table>
<tr><td>The Carter Family</td><td></td></tr>
<tr><td>Thomas Carter (Pa):</td><td>Pa works as a porter at Victoria Station. He is a quiet man, keeping his emotions to himself.</td></tr>
<tr><td>Mary Carter (Ma):</td><td>Ma works hard to keep her family clothed, fed and decently brought up at the family home in Sabine Road, Battersea. She worries about her children but is proud of those that head out to the Front.</td></tr>
<tr><td>Charles Carter:</td><td>Charlie is the eldest of the Carter children and a regular soldier with the British Expeditionary Force. He is on exercise in Ireland when war breaks out.</td></tr>
<tr><td>Edward Carter:</td><td>Ed works as a casual labourer and is something of a free-thinker and a rebel. He has no desire to fight in the war.</td></tr>
<tr><td>Rose Carter:</td><td>Rose is the third child and a trained nurse. She is intelligent, compassionate and strong-minded.</td></tr>
<tr><td>Walter Carter:</td><td>Walter was born in 1895, lives at home and works as a porter at Clapham Junction Station. He joined the Territorial Force (forerunner of the Territorial Army) in 1912 and because of that, is one of the first to be mobilised when war breaks out. A cheerful chap, he has the confidence of a young man who thinks the future is bright.</td></tr>
<tr><td>Annie Carter:</td><td>Annie is seven when the war breaks out. She suffers from infantile paralysis (Poliomyelitis) and has difficulty moving around. However, she is a bright and well-loved little girl.</td></tr>
</table>

Lily Howes:	Walter's girlfriend. She lives nearby and works behind the counter at Arding & Hobbs, the local departmental store in Battersea. She harbours a desire to be a teacher but for now she has to work wherever she can to help support her mother.
Mabel Green:	Lily's best friend. She also works at Arding & Hobbs. She is headstrong and a passionate supporter of the suffragettes.
Frederick Dickenson:	Fred is Walter's closest friend. He works at Clapham Junction Station with Walter and is also a member of the same Territorial Force battalion, 1/23rd (County of London) Battalion The London Regiment.
John Moore:	A school friend of Walter's, John is a member of the Royal Naval Reserve. He pays close attention to international affairs and is one of the more well-read and informed characters.
Mrs Margaret Wiggins:	The Carter family's neighbour on Sabine Road. A real busybody, she is a constant source of annoyance to Walter's mother.

March 1914

—— ◆ ——

12th March

Walter:
You won't believe what happened today at work. I was carrying cases to Platform 2 as normal when I heard a commotion from across the tracks. What do I see next but Fred Dickenson chasing hell for leather after five chickens, with a bunch of people chasing after him! Turns out he dropped a fancy-looking trunk, it burst open and out came these squawking birds. So I left my gentleman with his cases and set off at a lick down the station (Territorial training coming in useful!). It took us half an hour at least to round them all up and the tracks was covered in feathers. The Stationmaster was not pleased.

Fred:
Thanks for sharing that, mate... crikey, the things some folk bring on a train. Me hands is covered in scratches. Best place for them birds is on the kitchen table.

Lily:
Poor Fred!

Mary:
Shame you couldn't bring one home for the Sunday roast. Sounds like you earned it.

16th March

Walter:
Well done to my beautiful Lily Ann Howes for her fresh job at Arding and Hobbs, right on the crossroads by Clapham Junction – only a few steps from work, and from the drill hall. She'll be able to hear me ringing my porter's bell. Proud of you Lil – just don't go getting ideas from them flash ladies coming in for 'harem' pantaloons.

Mary:
Well done Lily; what a grand opportunity. All these independent young women, Walter! You'll have to make sure you treat her right else she'll give you the chuck...

Fred:
That's fine news. Are you not becoming a teacher now?

Lily:
Thanks everyone. Who knows, Lily Howes might become a fashionable lady after all! Fred, I still hope to go to training college, just maybe when I've got a bit more money.

Mabel:
Don't worry Walt, all that clobber's too dear to buy anyway. I should say we'll have a fine time! Mrs Reed ought to give me some time to show you what's what on Wednesday Lil – you'll be getting on alright in no time.

19th March

Walter:	Charlie, I saw a bit in the paper about the trouble over Irish Home Rule. You and the army boys wouldn't fight against our own lads in Ulster, would you? Seems daft to fight them for wanting to stay part of the United Kingdom.
Charles:	Sorry you haven't had a line from me little brother – been busy here in sunny Ireland… of course none of us wants a war with Ulster, just got to hope the government sees sense.
Walter:	Might be an early election because of this, so they might have to.
Charles:	Good news. Keep telling me what the papers are saying and what people think of us back in London.

21st March

Walter:	Charlie, the Express says 100 army officers have resigned over the Ulster issue – is that right? Says they're not going to serve against our countrymen. Brave chaps.
Charles:	That's right Walt – it's all anyone talks about over here. Wouldn't get your hopes up yet though, we hear they're still sending warships over here.

24th March

Mary:	Charles, Ed, Rose, Walter – have a look at your grown up little sister. She insisted on having her picture taken in town and now the photographer says he might put it up in the window of the studio. He let me help hold her and she sat up so nice you never would have known about her poor legs.

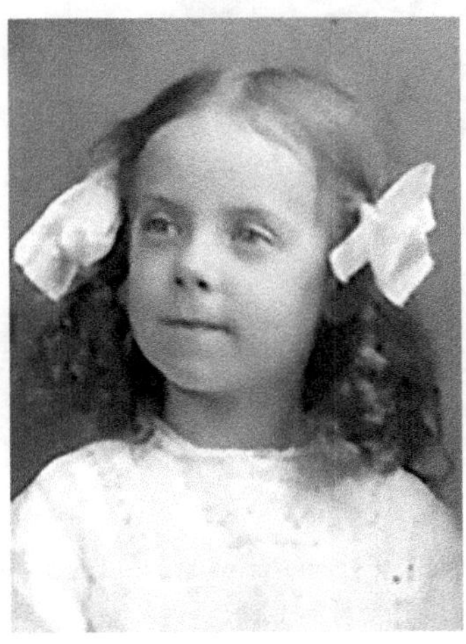

Charles:	Well that's a nice picture alright. I do miss you all and especially little Annie. She's so much bigger than when I was last at home. How's she getting on with her walking?
Rose:	Beautiful grown up girl. Tell Annie her big sister is going to kiss her all over that little face when I'm next at home.

Mary: She's going on alright with the walking, Charles, but only with my help and the sticks what Doctor Clarke gave us. She gets quite out of breath too, so we're careful, but I still tell your father I shan't think of having her sent to one of them schools for cripples.

Mabel: Didn't know you had a little sister as well as a big one Walt! Did she get the polio?

Walter: Yes, she got it when it went around that hot summer. Poor kid. Is it 'infantile paralysis' they call it Ma?

Mary: I'm afraid your father's not very pleased with us for discussing Annie in public… Mabel I would be glad if you didn't pass this on to your parents.

Mabel: I shan't say anything Mrs Carter.

27th March

Walter: You can bet I put a whole shilling on Sunloch to win The Grand National! That's 16 shillings in my pocket. I feel like a king. Nearly a week's wages! I could treat myself and Lily to a night in the stalls at the Grand or go to the Fox and Hounds with the lads and get pints of Burton all round… or give it to Ma for housekeeping. Decisions…

Ed: Get the Burton in, lad.

Mary: Don't listen to your brother, that's just the sort of thing he'd say. And me with 5 mouths to feed! We'll talk about this later, Walter.

Walter: Yes, Ma.

29th March

Walter:	Boys, there's plans to protest against the government sending forces to Ulster. Not sure when yet, but there's a march starting from Battersea so I'll be going even if I have to take a day off. I want the army to know we all support them – even us Territorials wouldn't think of going up there to fight.
Fred:	You're right there Walt, you wouldn't catch me fighting against our own. Hope the army can stick it. I ain't afraid to fight, mind – hopefully one day we'll get to use our training against a real enemy.
John:	Count me in. This scandal has made me sick. The papers said even the Germans think it's a rum job and the French don't know why we're fighting amongst ourselves.
Ed:	It's not going to make a bit of difference, Walt. Just tell the station you're going to go and then hook it for the day.
Mary:	Edward Carter, you're a toerag. Leave your brother alone, he's a good boy. Your father and I are very proud of you, Walter.

31st March

Walter:	What a fine day! Nice to have some sunshine at last. Making the best of it on the platforms at Clapham Junction but wish I was playing footie in the park with Fred and John… looking forward to TF training tonight though. Physical, so we might get to practise outside.
Fred:	At least you get to work in the sun, I'm on the wrong side of the platform all today.
Walter:	You'll be laughing when it rains… See you on parade at 7.

April 1914

◆

3rd April

Walter:	Just spotted the new London 'Wonderground' map at Waterloo. Me and Fred was having such a laugh at it that we nearly missed our train. Helps to take your mind off the overcrowding and cancellations anyway. Look out for our own Battersea Park at the bottom… and the boy getting eaten at London Zoo…

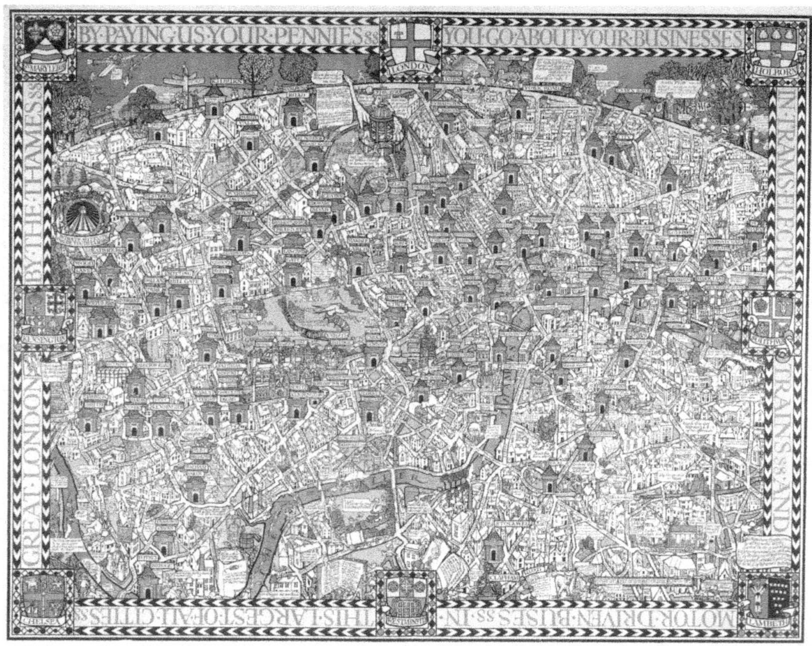

Fred:	Glad they got the cricket victory in… and the French pilot, "Have I looped yet?" Ha! Poor giraffe though.
Rose:	Funny to see Kennington Park Road on there – I cycle past the Oval every day on my way to the Infirmary.

4th April

Walter:	Well we have had a time of it – I never seen so many people. I was worried about taking Lily on a protest but it was alright, quite peaceful, and we all enjoyed ourselves despite the wet weather. 'Ballots not bullets!'
Charles:	Good show Walt! Good to hear everyone's on our side. Proud of you – maybe one day you'll make a real soldier like your big brother.
Walter:	You are a rum chap, just the other week we was doing field craft – if any war does come we'll be as ready as you are.

7th April

Walter: Ma always manages to make wonderful meals from the Sunday leftovers. For lunch today we had pig's fry with rice pudding for afters. What I'd give not to have to go back to work this afternoon… Ma, tell Annie to be a good little sister and save me some bread and dripping! Need my energy for training tonight.

9th April

Lily: Have you heard about 'The World, the Flesh and the Devil', Sweetheart? It's got a rotten title but they say it's "A £10,000 Picture Play in Actual Colours". Actual colours, Walt! They're showing it in town tonight. Hope it comes to the Imperial.

Walter: You just want to see Rupert Harvey in full colour.

Lily: Don't be jealous dear.

Walter: I'm just pulling your leg. I'll take you to see it when I've got some money. Gave most of me National winnings to Ma.

11th April

Walter: What a fine day out on Brighton beach with Lily! Even the weather held out for us. Nice to be on a train for once instead of portering. We had fun paddling in the sea and riding the donkeys. We even had ice-cream! I was pleased to get out of the city and away from the grime of Clapham Junction. We had such a grand time – it was a laugh seeing all the different people, from the chaps on the razzle-dazzle to the toffs in their bathing huts. All the girls looked lovely in their sailor suits – I ain't never seen so many legs on show! Not that I was looking…

12th April

Walter: Happy Easter pals! The whole family dressed up for church this morning (or as much as Ma can ever get Ed to dress up) and I spent all yesterday shining the buttons on me best uniform. Now I plan to spend the day eating as much food as I can get away with. Rose is home, helping Ma in the kitchen, and I must say it smells grand. It's little Annie's birthday as well, so I might even help her to paint some eggs later… 7 years old already…

April 1914

Mary: Annie's very excited now – she says you promised!

Lily: You did look handsome in your uniform, Walt. Proud to be walking out with a TF [Territorial Force] boy.

13th April

Walter: She said it! Mrs Campbell swore on a West End stage and the censors didn't do nothing about it. They say the audience laughed for more than a minute and the playwright walked out! I wish I'd seen it – I'll bet all the lads will be talking about it in the drill hall tomorrow.

14th April

Walter: Had the funniest night at training. We was on parade when Bert Hopkins makes a bad joke about Bill getting the drinks in the canteen after. Then Bill, he just can't help it, he pipes up in his best Eliza Doolittle voice, "Not b****y likely!" Well we all fell about, and the Commanding Officer went purple in the face. Poor old Bill couldn't get away with it of course – they asked him if he fancied leaving the TF, and it were all he could do not to say it again! But he just said, "I should think I'll stay then." Poor chap…

Mary: You watch your language!

15th April

Walter: Just heard about the train crash near Edinburgh. Sad day for the railway boys.

Lily: What happened?

Walter: The Flying Scotchman hit a goods train and went off the rails. The driver and fireman was killed and passengers hurt.

Lily: That's rotten news. I worry about you working with them machines… fast, loud, horrible things. Almost as dangerous as aeroplanes, I reckon.

Walter: You worry too much. It'll be a long time before I work me way up to anything like Engine Driver. The most risky thing about being a porter is dealing with all the people. They're more dangerous than any train…

16th April

Walter: Ma, the Express says one day all of London will be 'electrified'. You can bet it won't be for years, but imagine not having to get knocked about in the dark when you don't fancy wasting a candle! No oil lamps neither, no fancy gas lamps – not even gas lights in the streets. Heaven knows what Mr East will do for a job if there's no lamplighters no more. I should think it would be great at home though – they said they could even use it for heating and 'domestic purposes'.

Mary: What will they think of next? I don't know about this electricity.

Walter: I know Ma, but think what they mean about 'domestic purposes' – imagine if it could help with washday! I know you'd like that.

Mary: Well that would be a treat. If it could light the copper for me in the morning and save me lifting all them buckets of water then I'm all for it. Perhaps your 'electricity' could make me a cup of tea while it's at it…

17th April

Fred: See you for a game of darts this evening?

Walter: Great. Can't afford a beer anywhere outside the drill hall canteen at the minute so I'll see you up there. Would like to get in a game of shove ha'penny too.

21st April

Lily: What a day! We've sold out of parasols in Arding & Hobbs. Three days of good weather and everybody goes barmy on the crumpet. Mabel had a hilarious time trying to fit all them ladies for frocks.

Mabel: Funny for you! I had Mrs Reed breathing down me neck all day, not to mention when I came a cropper over the measuring tape.

Lily: I've never seen anything so funny. You should audition for the Keystone Cops!

23rd April

Walter:	All alright, Fred? Ed went past your house, said he could hear you cursing!
Fred:	I been practising doing up me puttees, Walt. I don't know how you gets them so neat every time. I spent half an hour trying to do it proper, turning the air blue the whole time, and gave up.

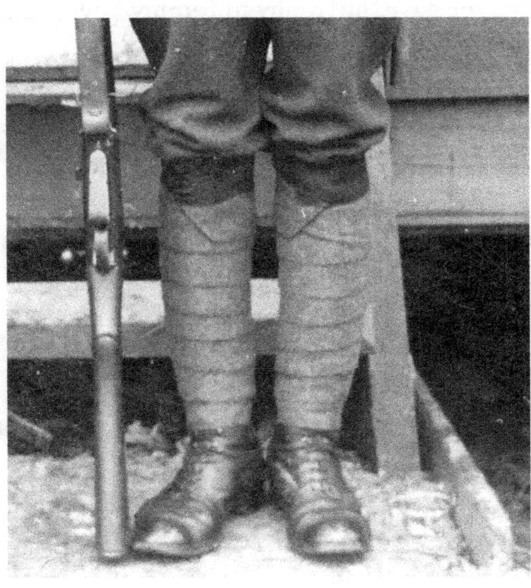

Walter:	You have to just do it slow, you can't rush it.
Fred:	If I went any slower it would take me an hour every time I wore me uniform!

25th April

Walter:	FA Cup Final at Crystal Palace today. Put a bet on down the drill hall bar last night. My money's on Liverpool to beat Burnley. At least these fellows have got a good view, eh?

Fred: Bad luck pal, 1-0 to Burnley. Jim said Arthur Metcalfe had a clean shot at goal for Liverpool but got the wind up him and missed the ball altogether!

Mary: Your father says the King was there, is he having me on Walter? He says it's the first time we've had a monarch at a football final. Imagine, a king amongst the common folk!

Walter: That's right, Ma. He even gave the trophy to Tommy Boyle. Seems a good sport.

27th April

Walter: Them suffragettes caused a bit of commotion up by the Serpentine… you remember when we walked up there Lily?

Lily: Of course I do! They had a show there today and some suffragettes swam out to the boats and cut them loose. Mabel says she wished she'd done it too but I don't know. I don't see how it's going to help. Like when Mary Thingamajig attacked that beautiful painting – all that happened then was that I couldn't go to the museums without a chaperone.

Walter: Just be safe, Lil. These women will get their way one way or another I'm sure.

Mabel: Mary Richardson! And of course it's going to help! I told you what Mrs Pankhurst said – people think it's 'hysteria' that 'takes the shape of irresponsible breaking of windows, burning of letters, general inconvenience' but if we can't vote then how else are we going to get people to listen? We'll let them know what we think 'rationally' when we get the vote.

May 1914

1st May

Walter: Well, what a change… I ain't seen a single person this morning who ain't said how cold it is. And May Day's meant to be the start of the good weather! Remember when we went to the Horse Parade in the park when we was children, Rose? Maybe it's just my memory but I'm sure it was always sunny then.

Mary: Annie says she's going to be May Queen one day, and that you can bet the sun will come out then. It breaks my heart to think how she'll never be able to dance around a maypole.

Rose: Just tell her she'll make a beautiful May Queen one day and to work hard on her walking, poor little one. Yes, Walt, I remember! You was only four and hid behind me because you was scared of the horses.

Walter: I think you're remembering it wrong.

5th May

Walter: Got worried reading about the 'Super-Tax' in the papers – they say it's 'War Taxes in Peace Time'.

Walter: Talked to the lads about it at training tonight – we reckon we'll still be paying 9d. in the pound on a £60 salary. If I ever earn more than £3,000 a year I'll have to pay the Super-Tax (1s 9d or more!)… how about that, Fred?

Fred: Not likely! Like I said, if we ever earn that sort of money I'm buying meself a motor.

7th May

Walter: Seems the Votes for Women Bill got a 'No' in the House of Lords. I'm sorry, Lily. You've still got my vote.

Lily: Hardly anyone thinks our wages would get better even if we did have a vote, so I suppose we've still got a long way to go. They'd never open it to an 18 year old woman anyway.

8th May

Walter: Blimey, have you seen the paper today? This French fellow Bachelet has invented a train that don't touch the rails. It floats, Fred. Magnets or something.

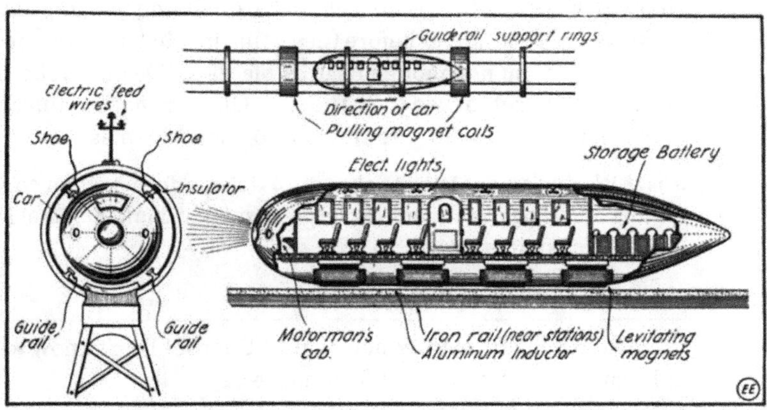

Fig. 2.—The 500 Mile Per Hour Electric Railway of the Future, Will Quite Likely Be of the Levitated Type, as Here Illustrated. Powerful Electro-Magnets Within the Car Raise It Above the Track, while Properly Spaced Solenoids Pull the Car Along.

Fred: I know, he says we could go from London to Brighton in 15 minutes! That sounds grand enough but what if they don't need no porters? And it's made out of metal and gets electrified. I don't know the science, but he sounds off his onion to me.

Walter: You'd never get my mother on one – she'd think she was going to get electrified as well. 15 minutes to Brighton though, that would be something. I should like to drive one. Although think how long it takes them to set up anything in this station – I reckon we're alright for a few years yet.

Walter: They say Winston Churchill went to see the model today. He said, "It is the most wonderful thing I have ever seen... By George, it's great!" Although I don't know if I'd trust anything the First Lord of the Admiralty says, not after the Ulster scandal.

9th May

Walter:	Rose, Lily says they had a smart doctor in the shop today and he was on about making a cure for cancer – thought you might know something about it, being a nurse.
Rose:	Yes, it happened at Lambeth Lily, where I work. The cancer was in the girl's neck but it went down when they put radium on it. It's a big discovery – don't know if it will work for everyone, mind. The best thing would be a cure for consumption as most of the cases we gets from the workhouse next door has that.
Lily:	Do you see a lot from the workhouse?
Rose:	Oh, most of them! The workhouse may as well be an infirmary what with all the sick people there. A lot gets sick from living in damp and dirty lodgings or on the street before they come in. That's London for you – too many people and not enough healthy places to live in. Lambeth's the worst of it… I hope I get moved to St Thomas'. Glad I'm not a trainee nurse no more though, having to give all them soft soap enemas…
Mary:	Rose! We don't want to hear about it. I'll never forget when you was talking about bed baths out in the garden and I could just feel Mrs Wiggins listening next door.

10th May

Walter:	Happy birthday from the whole family, Charlie! Don't know what you do in Ireland for a birthday, but have a nice day.

May 1914

| Mary: | Happy birthday, son. We all miss you and look forward to when we can have the whole family together again. Your father sends his regards. |
| Charles: | Thanks everyone. As ever, it's a strange thing to have me birthday and not be at Sabine Road. I daren't think about the puddings you used to make for me, Ma, they make me want to pack up and get on a boat home! |

12th May

Walter:	Enjoyed ourselves very much at training tonight. Band was practising in the hall so all quite cheerful. Boots are wearing out a bit though.
Fred:	Says the juggins who wears his uniform boots to work...
Walter:	I ain't got no others! Except me walking-out ones, and I keeps them for best. You remember when you said I should join and you told me about the 'free boots'? Well, that's what did it, Fred. I'm getting as much wear out of these boots as I can.

16th May

Walter:	We have had a fine day. Packed up work at noon, same as any other Saturday. Then the whole company in best suits set off to see the Royal Naval and Military Tournament at Olympia. I'd say it's better than any show I ever saw... most particularly the galloping of the guns and the rough-riding by the Artillery men. Made me proud to be a military man and I should think any enemy seeing that would turn right around and go home. Big show about 'The Romans in Britain' too, with chariots and spears and arrows. Funny to think that's how people used to fight.
John:	I should like to see that – the boys in the Navy say the gun drill's very good.
Fred:	See if you can get along, John. It'll make you proud alright.

20th May

Mary:	Your father read that a railwayman in Tamworth saved a baby from a train – Annie asked if it was you, Fred! I explained it would take you a fair time to walk to Tamworth for work. They say the baby crawled onto the tracks and he scooped it up just as a train came by.
Fred:	That's the nature of a railwayman, Mrs Carter. Heroic to the last. Funny she thought it was me, not you, Walt...
Walt:	He's cheeking me, Ma... Put us to the test and we'll see who's a hero.

22nd May

Walter: Well Lily, ain't you glad I told you not to go on that suffragette march now?

Lily: I know, I'm sorry I was cross with you. Mabel came into work this morning looking very tired and when she showed me her arms they was black and blue. She was trying to get past the policemen near Buckingham Palace but they had truncheons and beat her. She said Mrs Pankhurst nearly got to the Palace with her petition for the King but she got carried off. I think she must've been arrested.

Ed: The papers are right about them wild women. Don't get caught up with them Lil.

Mabel: I'll keep saying it, if we can't vote then we have to find other ways. It's not 'wild' or 'disgraceful' or whatever else the Express says, it's just necessary. 'Deeds not words!'

Charles: For once in me life, I think I'm with Ed on this. I don't see how these women think they're going to get anywhere by behaving like fiends. 'Votes for Women', that's one thing, but violence in women just ain't right. Don't put yourself in danger, Lily.

Lily: I don't know what to think. I shouldn't like to be beaten, but I don't think it's fair that we can't vote.

Walter: I'm just glad you ain't hurt, sweetheart. Keep out of trouble and things will work out sooner or later, I'm sure.

23rd May

Lily: More news today: a woman tried to give a speech about votes for women to the King at His Majesty's Theatre. The Express article did make me feel unsettled, it kept calling her 'it' instead of 'she'.

25th May

Walter: Home Rule's been passed! Ireland are going to get their own parliament. Couldn't make much sense of the news in the papers but I think it ain't over yet, and they might let Ulster stay part of Britain for 6 years as a test.

Rose: Pa says the House of Commons agreed but it's happened twice before and it never gets through the House of Lords. I suppose we'll see what happens – the Lords can't do much now anyway.

27th May

Walter: The ice is melting for Derby Day today (it was colder than Norway yesterday – couldn't get warm at training)! I hope the King's horse gets through this year with no suffragettes getting in the way. Fred says they've put up extra barriers and there's policemen around the course, so it should all go off well. Kennymore's the favourite – I'm thinking of putting a little on him to see if my luck from the Grand National holds out. What do you think, Ed?

Ed: Hard to tell, but Kennymore looks a good bet – did well at Newmarket. Quite young.

Mary: Go careful with your money, Walter. Now that Lily has her own job she won't want to be seen with a fellow on the doss…

Walter: I'm lucky, Ma. I wouldn't back it if I didn't think it was a winner.

28th May

Walter: Well, what bad luck with the Derby. Hardly anyone had heard of the horses what finished first, second and third… one of them was 100 to 1! Whoever put money on that's a lucky chap. Kennymore was nowhere after delaying the start and then getting away badly. Don't worry, Ma, Lil, I didn't put too much on.

Mary: That'll teach you to listen to your brother.

Fred: It's alright, didn't Bert Hopkins take a wild bet on Durbar II at 20-1? We won't let him forget it if he did. Drinks on Hopkins at the Terrier social tomorrow night boys!

30th May

Fred: Another steam ship disaster, Walt. First the Titanic, then the Columbian, now the Empress of Ireland. A lot of the crew was saved this time but they're saying more passengers died than what was on the Titanic… You can bet I'm glad we work on the railways, not the ships. If I ever leave England, I'm going in an aeroplane.

John: Good job you're not with us in the Navy! Aeroplanes are far worse – Hamel the aviator's still missing, isn't he?

June 1914

◆

1st June

Walter: The Germans are going to have a show of 'aerial combat' in Mainz, near Berlin – what I'd give to see that! Aeroplanes, balloons and Zeppelins on a practice mission, with codes written on them for the 'enemy' to work out. Imagine wars being fought in the sky… that would be a thrill.

Mary: Thrill, my eye! If they were the enemy and could fly over here with bombs to drop on Battersea, you wouldn't talk such footle. Be careful what you wish for.

Fred: It's alright Mrs Carter, the Germans can play with their Zeppelins, it's Ireland we're worrying about. And if the enemy gets anywhere near Battersea, the 23rd London Regiment will make them wish they'd never got out of bed!

4th June

Fred: Walter, John – looks like it's England's turn now. Our boys had a go at dropping bombs out of aeroplanes over Salisbury Plain. Only paper ones, mind, but the marksmen were so good they could hit a tent on the ground from up in the air! The paper said all of Salisbury would have been wiped out if it hadn't been make-believe. Well done lads.

Walter: That is impressive. I'll almost be bored having to practise on the ground at training on Tuesday…

8th June

Walter: Happy Birthday, Freddy! Somehow you always manage to sneak in a birthday two days before mine. We'll have to sing you that new song – ask Annie what it is, Ma, I know the children sing it sometimes.

Mary: Annie's singing it to you from here, Fred!
Happy birthday to you
Happy birthday to you
Happy birthday dear Fred
Happy birthday to you!

Fred: Well, thank you very much! Tell Annie I'm very pleased with it.

9th June

Walter: Every day now there's something in the paper about them suffragettes... wherever the King and Queen go they get a woman telling them about force feeding in the prisons, or torture, or voting... they must get right fed up. Bert was on parade tonight, says his sisters only wear green, purple and white now – suffragette colours.

Charles:	Sounds like an epidemic of madwomen… we ought to forget the Ulstermen and the Germans and sort the women out first, before the whole of England turns lunatic.
Mabel:	Quite right too – sort us out with the vote.
Lily:	Oh Mabel, I don't think that's what he meant. Nice to hear the Queen say something about it though – I was expecting her to be angry but she just said, "If this had been the worst thing the women had done they might perhaps be forgiven." I wonder if she's secretly on our side after all.

10th June

Lily:	Happy birthday, sweetheart! I've had a new photographic portrait taken and I plan to make a present of it, what do you think?
Walter:	Thank you Lily, I think that would be just wonderful. I should like to have a little picture of you to keep with me.
Mary:	You two! Imagine if your father saw such a public show. You'll see Lily soon enough for a celebration I'm sure, Walter. In the meantime, I've made your favourite meat pudding for dinner and we even have a cake that Annie helped to make. It does look the part.
Walter:	Thanks, Ma.

11th June

Walter:	Where was it you went for your photograph, Lily? I just saw Mayor John Archer coming out of his photographic studio on Battersea Park Road. It still surprises me that he manages to keep up his business and be Mayor at the same time.
Ed:	Hardly the most surprising thing about him though, is it?

Walter: You mean because of his colour? That's just Battersea for you – if anywhere was going to elect the first black mayor in London, you can bet it was going to be Battersea! Not everyone's cup of tea, but he's doing a lot for the poor.

Lily: His place was closed, so I went up the one by Clapham Common. My Ma says Mayor Archer's studio is closed more often than not while he's doing council business.

Charles: I heard he was from Rangoon or India or somewhere. See, I knew some Hindus when we was in India and I would say he don't look like them.

Walter: No, that's just what the papers said when he wouldn't tell them where he was from. When he got in he said he was actually from Liverpool…

Rose: It was a good speech he gave. Look out for the sarcasm… "I am the son of a man who was born in the West Indian islands. I was born in England, in a little obscure village that probably never was known until this evening… the City of Liverpool. I am a Lancastrian born and bred, and my mother – well she was my mother. She was not born in Rangoon and she was not Burmese. She belonged to one of the greatest races on the face of the earth. My mother was an Irishwoman, so there is not much of the foreigner about me after all."

14th June

Walter: What a storm! Thunder and lightning like it's the end of the world.

Lily: We have hailstones the size of half-crowns coming down in our street. The cats are crazed and it's set all the dogs off barking. The little'uns are pretending to be scared but I'm quite enjoying meself! The road looks like a branch of the Thames…

Crowds gather to witness the flooding in Mitcham.

Blood-Red Tempest
South London
14th June 1914

Lily: Mabel, I've just thought about you and your family all in that basement flat on Shelgate Road. Let me know if you're getting on alright.

Lily: Send us a line if you can, Mabel.

Mabel: Sorry about that, we was all sitting down to eat our Sunday dinner when mother gave a yell that the water was coming down the steps and we spent the next hour trying to stop it getting in. Little brother was pretending he was aboard the Empress of Ireland, which didn't help no one, and we ended up with two inches of water in the flat. Have been doing our best to bail it out but Pa says we'll have to stay with Aunt Florence up the road for a while.

Lily: That's horrible, I'm so sorry. Come to visit if you need to. Glad to hear you're alright though.

Walter: Ma and I are sorry to hear it, Mabel. If you need any help with the flat I'll bring the boys over. How is it at the Lodging House, Rose?

Mabel: Thank you, you're good pals.

Rose: Alright here. My cubicle's near the top of the house anyway. Edie and I spent the storm shouting to each other over the partition!

15th June

Lily: Oh how sad to hear about the children hit by lightning on Wandsworth Common. They should know better than to stand under a tree in a storm, but poor dears.

Walter: Did you see what happened to the lady's hat? We'd better stay inside for training tomorrow – imagine 100 men with bayonets in that lightning!

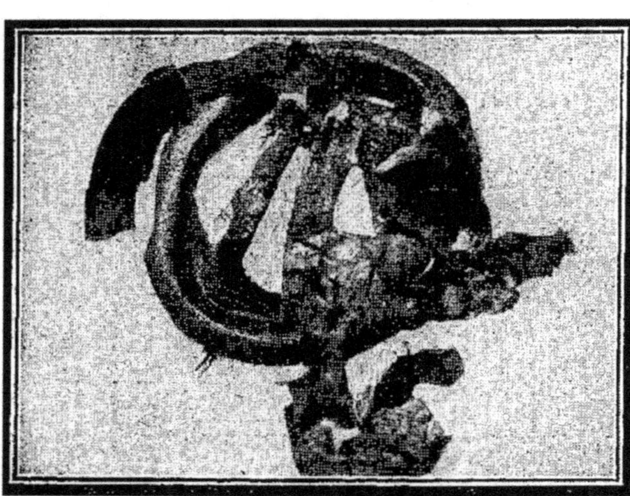

All that remained of the hat of the woman who was killed.

Lily: Don't you even joke about it!

17th June

Walter:	Ascot races today! Wish I could take you there, Lily.
Lily:	Everyone at Arding & Hobbs has been talking about what all the ladies will wear. Thank heavens the weather is better. We've had people asking for all sorts of exotic things in the shop: transparent skirts even, so you can see their ankles and shins! There are parasols in different shapes, with the handles off to one side when you open them. Quite a good idea I should say.
Mabel:	Don't forget the 'Futurist' black and white shoes!

Lily:	Of course, and the flash jewelled ones – and the hats with the enormous feathers...

18th June

Walter:	Yet more travel upsets. A German liner and another Liverpool steam ship crashed and the Bristol train to Ascot hit the Great Western express train at Reading. The express driver died but I'm surprised no one else did... seven out of eight coaches had their sides ripped clean off. I reckon the signalman got fuddled, eh Fred?
Fred:	I suppose he did. It's that sort of mistake the new signal lad gets nightmares about. Don't like to think about it meself neither.

19th June

Walter: That weren't the end of it, what I said yesterday. The paper says today about a Scottish train what fell into a river, a German liner getting onto rocks by Portland Bill, another German ship crashing in the channel, a British steamship wrecked near Africa and then one in the Philippines. And the fire in the dock at Glasgow burning four ships. All yesterday. Something's wrong with the world.

Ed: There was more lightning too, up in the Midlands. It killed a man and two horses, and everything's flooded.

John: Civil war starting in Albania as well – wouldn't think nothing of it, only they've just sent 100 of our Marines to guard the prince. My Pa says the world's like a pot about to boil, says the European countries are fighting over who gets to start a war first.

THE BOILING POINT.

Fred: All them countries is always fighting against each other. Nothing to do with us, I say.

Lily: Seems we're more likely to get hit by lightning than a bomb. Two more people killed in storms today… I'm frightened to go out of the house! Especially having to take a brolly.

20th June

Walter: Here, John, it looks like the British and Russian Navies have been getting very cosy, toasting each other… so I suppose Russians will be on our side if anything does come our way. They've been arming and reorganising their military too, so should be top notch.

John: Good to know, although I heard they've still got 2 years before they're fully armed. Not that our boys would need any help.

Walter: The Terriers are ready for anything too.

21st June

Walter: What a lousy Sunday. One piece of homemade shortbread each and I drop mine in me tea.

Fred: Ha! Bad luck Walt.

22nd June

Walter: Well, now the Austrians have tried their hand at an aerial combat show, but made a rum job of it. A biplane flew over an airship as if to drop bombs on it but it caught the balloon with the propeller. Both went down in flames. I wouldn't have thought Austria-Hungary would try it again. They want to come here and see it done proper.

23rd June

Walter: Talk at up the drill hall tonight about a civil war with Ireland. Ulster wants to stay part of us for more than just 6 years, but Asquith's government don't look like they're going to agree. Can't see the sense of it at all, not after the army have said they won't fight against the Ulster boys.

Fred: I know we'd all like a chance to use our training, but not like this. Waste of an army that'd be.

24th June

John: Have you seen the new air force badge in the paper? Proud to say the Royal Naval Air Service is now going to be a service by itself. The emblem is going to be an eagle. Good choice, eh Walter?

Walter: Sounds grand. They'll still need us on the ground though… You should have seen us at training last night – even Fred kept time!

Fred: I never was much for rhythm, was I? Could still stick it to the enemy though, whoever he turns out to be. Great badge, John.

25th June

Rose:
Looks like you were right about dangerous umbrellas Lily… a German chap was caught in one of these thunderstorms –he got away from the trees and laid himself down in the middle of a field, but opened his brolly to keep off the rain, and the lightning hit it! Four other people killed by lightning in Europe too. I should think I'd rather get rained on.

Lily:
I knew it! Everyone's been buying umbrellas and parasols at the shop because the weather keeps changing. I think they should come with a warning.

SOME THOUGHTS ABOUT JUNE WEATHER.

27th June

Walter:
Just so that everyone knows, the porter called 'Walter' who was nearly hit by a train wasn't me, it was some other chap, a Walter Simpson, from Godalming. Silly fellow was carrying parcels across the line and didn't see the express coming through until it was nearly on top of him! He jumped up onto the platform just in time (army training) and only the heel of his boot was knocked off. Not to mention there's been another train crash – Cannon Street this time.

Mary:
Just you be careful.

Walter:
I nearly didn't say nothing because I knew you'd fret! Don't worry, I'm smarter than that… and I'm enjoying life far too much to put meself in danger, eh Lily?

Lily:
Glad to hear it! Are you still taking me to the music hall tonight?

Walter:
Of course I am – I been saving up me TF Bounty Night pay so I got plenty to make a grand time of it at the Grand! I'll put on me walking-out uniform and we'll be the finest couple there.

Mary:	Enjoy yourselves. And behave.

28th June

Walter:	There's rumours going about that the Austrian Archduke and his wife have been murdered in Bosnia. Will have to see what the papers say tomorrow.
Charles:	Rum news. Could be trouble if it's true.

29th June

Walter:	The papers are full of it today, about the assassination of Archduke Franz Ferdinand. Take a look at the article. A chap my age shot him and his wife with a Browning pistol. Someone tried earlier in the day with a bottle bomb full of nails but it bounced off the car. Anyone know what this is all about? John?
John:	Well, Bosnia is occupied by Austria-Hungary, and Pa says the Archduke was over there inspecting the Austrian army…

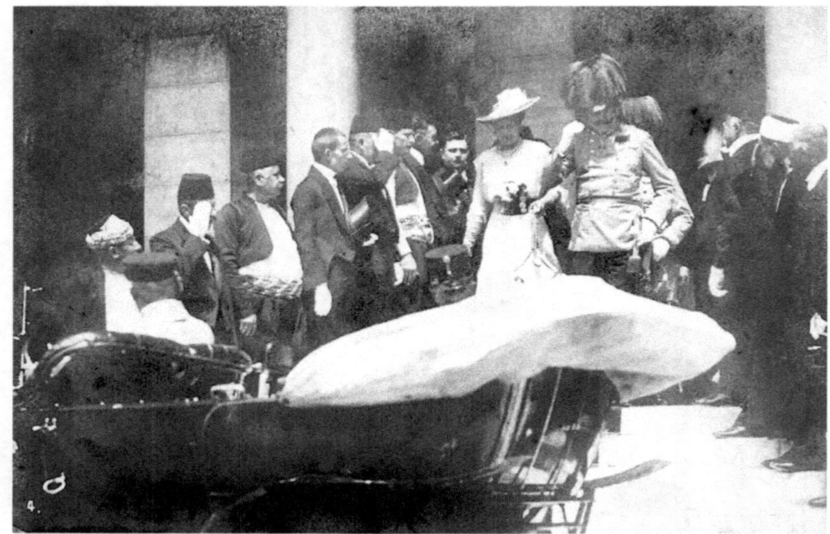

Rose: The assassin was Serbian though, so you can bet Austria-Hungary's going to come down hard on Serbia over this. I reckon Germany would back them up too.

Walter: Bad idea to get the wind up them, looks like they've been preparing for war anyway. Let them face us Terriers, they won't know what hit them.

Fred: Still don't see what it has to do with us. They can sort each other out. I'm going home for me dinner.

July 1914

———◆———

1st July

Walter: Well, you can always rely on England for a sudden change in the weather… 90 degrees in the shade it is. A bit trying when you're rushing between trains, but fine after work in the long evenings. And I always like to see the girls with their parasols. Someone said the river at the Henley Regatta looks like a field of multi-coloured mushrooms because of the sun shades.

Fred: It is just about impossible to sleep though. I always look forward to a heatwave but get fed up when it comes. The Daily Mirror says some people have taken to sleeping outside. Sounds alright to me. Anyway, Walt, here's a picture you might like, but it'll make you wish you lived by the seaside – a bunch of lovely young ladies (ignore the fellows) gone for a midnight swim to cool off.

Walter: I must say I'm very pleased with that.

2nd July

Lily: Mabel and I was having a wonderful discussion at Arding & Hobbs today. She said soon we'll be able to telephone to America over the wireless, or even fly to New York itself in an airship! It sounds wonderful, but I shouldn't like to fly in this weather. It looks like the thunderstorm has broken the heatwave, but there's been two more people killed by lightning…

Walter: I heard about the experiment, although, to be frank Lil, it just looked like a boat with an aeroplane stuck on it… and it could only get up for a few seconds before coming back down again because of all the weight – it had 10 people on board! The wireless telephone though, well that is something. They say it'll be possible to telephone to New York before the end of the year, but the wireless company thinks we won't ever be able to call from home.

Another fascinating possibility was opened up when Sir H. Rider Haggard asked if it would ever be possible for a man to telephone from his own house to any part of the world.

"I would not like to go so far as that at present," said Mr. Isaacs. "I do not quite see how certain difficulties can be got over. I think it will be possible to go to a particular station in London and telephone to New York, but I do not think it would be easy for any one to telephone from his office to New York."

"In short," said Sir Henry, "all the wireless business stands at present on the threshold of unrevealed things."

3rd July

Lily: This made me chuckle – I thought we could use a bit of light news…
'Wimbledon weather' again at the tennis. I'm half glad we're not there with the toffs after all!

3rd July

Walter: Well, now Germany has submarines with six-inch guns attached and extra torpedo tubes…

John: Don't worry about it, Walt. The Germans and Russians have got the biggest vessels, but our Navy is the best in the world.

5th July

Walter: RIP Joseph Chamberlain, 'The Apostle of Empire'. Passed away on Thursday. I reckon the government today could learn a lot from him. I liked what he said:

"It is not a good policy to say nothing of morality – it is not a good policy to sit upon a fence."

Rose:	"We cannot hold our own unless, like our fathers, we are open to new ideas."
John:	"My first proposal is that we should treat the foreigners as they treat us. My second proposal is that we should treat our friends better than we treat our opponents."
Walter:	"We must draw closer together, or we shall drift apart."

8th July

| Mary: | They're having an inquiry into all these train crashes. Thought you might like to know. |
| Walter: | Thanks, Ma. The 'Engineer' chap who wrote to the Express said exactly what me and Fred have been saying – that there's just not enough guards on the trains. That's what happens when they don't put the money into it. One guard has to do everything, so he ends up clerking and sorting luggage at the back of the train when he should be at the front checking signals and making sure the driver ain't lost his head. |

Mary:	Mrs Wiggins next door made a comment about how it's a porter's job to sort luggage. I told her she wouldn't of course understand the work of railways, being that her husband works in 'business'.
Walter:	Ignore her. Luggage is my business when it's on the platform, the guard's when it's on the train.
Fred:	Hope the inquiry makes a change. Me and Walt always says they ought to have a head guard up the front to pull the brake if there's an emergency. As long as they don't pay him with a cut from our wages, that is.

10th July

Walter:	You know you was saying about all the ladies in the shop wanting 'hobble skirts', Lily? Well, they're thinking of making stiles v-shaped so women can get over them on country walks! Did make me chuckle when I thought of it. Then I read that v-shaped stiles wouldn't work after all because stout people couldn't get through them. Fred and I had a laugh picturing it. I like the way the skirts look, but you'd have to get the sort with buttons else I wouldn't have thought you could walk…

THE HOBBLE SKIRT.

"WHAT'S THAT? IT'S THE SPEED-LIMIT SKIRT!"

11th July

Walter:	More suffragette action, in Scotland this time.
Lily:	I know. One poor lady nearly died trying to get close to the King's car to speak to him, and another with a placard saying 'visit the torture chamber in Perth Prison' had a jug of water poured on her head from a window.
Walter:	Didn't know there was still torture chambers… sounds a bit off.
Mabel:	Don't be soft, there are women being tortured every day in the prisons.
John:	Don't listen Walt, she means forced feeding of the suffragettes on hunger strike. The guards have got to make sure they eat somehow and it's their own fault if they won't let it.
Mabel:	It's the only way they can protest! You ought to hear them describe it, it's awful.

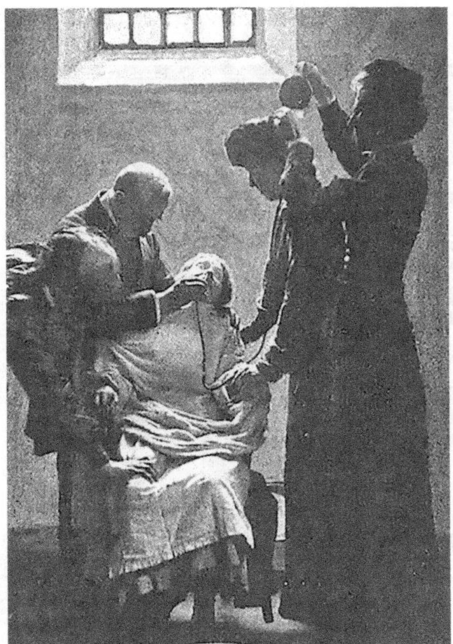

13th July

Walter: Charlie, reckon you might've seen this – armed Unionist volunteers in Ulster on Saturday. They had a speech from their leader, Sir Edward Carson – there's "no hope of peace," he said, unless it's "peace with honour". Good on him. Looks like we're heading into a civil war in your beloved Ireland though. No European war after all as Franz Ferdinand's father is the Austrian Emperor and he's put his foot down on that.

Charles: That's right. The House of Lords made some changes to the Home Rule Bill too, saying it should be for all of Ulster, not just part, and for more than 6 years. The Nationalists won't take that well.

The volunteers raise cheers for their leader, Sir Edward.

Charles: The Nationalists have had their own volunteer march now. 4,000 of them…

Watching the march past. The men belong to Meath, Louth and Monaghan.

Walter: The paper says there's more than 100,000 altogether. I'd say you have rough times ahead.

14th July

Walter: Always pleased to use me Long Lee Enfield at training, even if we don't have the Short Magazine like the regulars. Just wish we got to actually fire them more as I'm fed up with practising. The War Office ought to give us more money for ammunition – five rounds a year ain't enough for anyone.

15th July

Walter: 'Contest of the century' tonight boys! Didn't talk of nothing else at training yesterday. White Heavyweight Champion… Carpentier vs Gunboat Smith. I'm putting a bit on Carpentier the Frenchman – did you see the fuss everyone made when he arrived in London? The crowd undid the horses from his carriage and pulled it up the Strand themselves.

Fred: I'm behind Carpentier too. His manager says he eats lions for breakfast, tigers for lunch and elephants for dinner! Come with me down the Fox and Hounds this evening and we'll get Jim to put us a bet on.

Ed: Beats me why you'd back a Frenchman over an American.

Fred: The English and the French are rivals alright, but when it's something as important as this we tend to come over all neighbourly.

16th July

Walter: Well that was lucky. Carpentier was on his knees and my sixpence nearly wasted, when Gunboat gave him a foul blow and was disqualified. They took a complete cinematograph of the fight too. I should like to see it.

Fred: A lucky escape I say. The cinematograph shows every hit – they're showing pictures of it in the paper.

18th July

Walter: A few bits of news from Europe recently: France has asked for £56 million for weapons… (imagine 56 MILLION POUNDS, Fred!) And Germany flew a Zeppelin over the Russian frontier this morning. The Russians shot at it but it escaped. Not sure what to make of it.

John:
I shouldn't think Britain will get involved if anything does happen, maybe just the Navy. We're too busy with Ireland. This is how it stands: Germany says they'll support Austria-Hungary if they choose to attack Serbia over the assassination, but Russia will back Serbia, then France will back Russia and I suppose we might end up backing France. But we're a few countries away from the real fighting.

21st July

Walter:
Any news on Ulster, Charlie?

Charles:
Not good news… they say it's "settlement or civil war in ten days, and probably civil war." Just heard more from one of the boys: Unionist leader Carson has made it all clear – unless Ulster is allowed to be completely separate from the Irish parliament and can stay part of Britain, it's war.

Walter: Our Captain says they're not even talking about it in the House of Commons anymore, just having meetings behind closed doors at Buckingham Palace. You ready for war, Charlie?

Charles: I'm a soldier Walt, I live for it. Just don't like to fight against our own Irish brothers, that's all.

22nd July

Walter: Even the King's on Ulster's side – look what he said: "We have in the past endeavoured to act as a civilising example to the world, and to me it is unthinkable, as it must be to you, that we should be brought to the brink of fratricidal strife upon issues apparently so capable of adjustment as those you are now asked to consider, if handled in a spirit of generous compromise." Can't understand all of it, but I think he wants them to step back and give Ulster what they want, easy. Beats going to war with our own countrymen anyway.

Fred: Hear hear, Your Majesty.

24th July

Walter: It's been nice this week to see all the kids around, with the schools finished for the holidays. Makes a railwayman's life more difficult… but it's better for Annie to have children her own age at home during the day, even if she can't play at skipping and Knock Down Ginger with them.

25th July

Walter: Well no one knows where to look now… the left hand side of the paper's telling us that the meetings with Ireland have failed and there's going to be a war, and the right hand side's telling us that the meetings with Serbia have failed and there's going to be a war.

Fred: I think everyone knows Ireland's the one to worry about. All that happens with foreign wars is the army goes over there, sorts it out and comes home again. If us Territorials get involved it'll be with Ireland, not Europe.

Mary: I should think so too. I've already got one son away on army duty and I didn't let you join the Terriers so you could go off and join him, Walter!

Walter: I know… Anyway, we Territorials ain't supposed to go abroad, that's what Charles's British Expeditionary Force is for. Shame really, I should like to see another country.

26th July

Walter:

A Belgian has won the Tour de France! Well done Philippe Thys. No one paid too much attention to the start of it because it was the same day the Archduke was assassinated…

27th July

John:

Very strange things going on today. Serbia replied to the ultimatum from Austria-Hungary saying they'd do everything they asked, apart from one thing: Austria wanted to come into Serbian territory to find out about the assassination, but Serbia said they'd do it themselves. That's it. Even the German Kaiser thought it meant peace, but now Austria-Hungary says the reply's not good enough… looks like they're going to declare war on Serbia after all.

July 1914

Walter:	Thanks John. It's all over the front page now and Ireland is off to the side…
Charles:	Don't write off Ireland – Nationalists and Unionists have clashed here. 4 people dead and about 60 injured.

28th July

Walter:	Looks like Britain's saved the day… Sir Edward Grey (our Foreign Secretary) has stepped in to get France, Germany and Italy to talk it over with Austria-Hungary and Russia. Bit of news from the Express: 'Unless Austria is determined to make war at all costs, the peace of Europe will be maintained.' Everything's gone calm and boring again.

Ed:	What good is talking now? Left it too late I reckon.
Rose:	For once, Pa says Ed has a point. The paper says how things are calming down, but down at the bottom there's a piece about a telegram from Austria-Hungary – says they plan to attack Serbia immediately. I'll bet you didn't see that.

29th July

Walter:	Rose, you had the truth of it. Austria-Hungary declared war on Serbia yesterday.
Fred:	Looks like the French were pretty happy about it – they were out on them boulevards cheering and singing!

> **WAR DECLARED BY AUSTRIA.**
>
> ---
>
> **HOSTILITIES COMMENCED**
>
> ---
>
> **SEIZURE OF A SERVIAN STEAMER.**
>
> ---
>
> **THE POWERS AND PEACE**
>
> ---
>
> **HOPES OF LOCALISING HOSTILITIES.**

Rose:	Not all of them, Fred… some were shouting, "Down with war".
Walter:	Cowards they'll be. I'm with the cheerers and singers – if we're going to war, let's go into it proud.
Fred:	Too right.
Mabel:	I'll bet no one's paying attention to the Bill in the House of Lords today – to make the grounds for divorce that apply to women apply to men.
Mary:	From the Express today – "The Six Great Powers find themselves ranged in two Titanic camps – that of the Triple Alliance: Austria, Germany and Italy; and that of the Triple Entente: France, Russia and Great Britain. If these armies are brought into play 10,000,000 men will be engaged in war." Have to say I got the shivers when I saw that.

30th July

Walter:	Alright, enough war talk. Who's ready for Terrier camp this Sunday? Two weeks away! Can't wait to live under canvas. The pay will be useful too.
Fred:	Ready in spirit but not stuff, Walt. Everything what's been happening has made me itch to get on with training, but these boots just ain't up to it and you know how bad I am at packing.
Walter:	Ma's doing all mine for me. Freshly ironed uniform and everything. She spent all Tuesday doing it. Got me old kit bag out too. You want to get yourself round here, Fred!
Mary:	I'll be glad to get rid of you for a while, with all the extra washing and ironing I've had to do!
Ed:	You wait, she'll be pining for you by Monday.
Mary:	Well I shall be stuck here with just your father, little Annie and her layabout brother.
Ed:	Told you.

August 1914

———◆———

1st August

Walter: Off to Salisbury Plain for training camp in the morning! Pleased to get out of Battersea for a while. Though I shall miss you, Lily Howes.

Lily: Oh go on, you soft thing! Have a good time.

2nd August

Walter: On our way to camp but the train has stopped between Willesden Junction and Acton. Not sure what's going on. Some of the boys are saying Bill left his pack on the station and the CO's making him run all the way back to Clapham Junction for it!

Walter: For some reason we've started pulling back towards home now… If this is all for Bill's pack I'll wallop him meself.

Walter: Well, it was nothing to do with Bill at all. We been told to go home for now but to be ready to report at short notice. Got a shiver when I heard that. I reckon we know what's coming. Training on Wimbledon Common from tomorrow until we hear any news.

Fred: Can't say I'm not excited – might see some real action! Better than pretending up Salisbury Plain.

Mary: I'll be glad to have you home, everyone's very nervous here.

John: If Germany don't stay out of Belgium, it'll be war for sure. Better be ready, boys!

3rd August

Walter: Germany has declared war on Russia. The Daily Mirror said, "It is Armageddon."

It is Armageddon. Germany has declared war on Russia and, it was reported yesterday, is massing troops on the French frontier. Britain is taking its holiday under a sense of appalling calamity and of impending destruction which makes one shudder to contemplate. On Saturday the Kaiser made a warlike speech, and said, "The sword is being thrust into our hand." Then the die was cast and London heard the dread news at supper time. The War Lord is seen wearing the uniform of the "Death's Head Hussars." The postcard, which has an enormous sale shows a German and an Austrian soldier standing side by side. The inscription means "Let them all come."

4th August

Walter: Got me identity disc stamped today and me field service pay book sorted. I need to keep that safe (right hand breast pocket) as it's got all me details in. No declaration of war yet but we're preparing for mobilisation. All very exciting.

Charles: Us too. There's some talk of us holding off going to France until you Terriers are mobilised… but I reckon we'll be going anyway.

Mabel: Saw a mobilisation notice come up on the cinema screen tonight. Walter, Fred, looks like you have to report tomorrow.

Walter: I saw it too, Mabel, on a notice at the station. Here we go, Fred!

Lily: Do you know where you'll be going? Will you visit me first?

Walter: I shouldn't think we'll be off anywhere just yet, Lil. There'll be a lot to do here before that.

5th August

Walter: Well lads, we are at war! Announcement from last night:

"Owing to the summary rejection by the German Government of the request made by His Majesty's Government for assurances that the neutrality of Belgium would be respected, His Majesty's Ambassador in Berlin has received his passport, and His Majesty's Government has declared to the German Government that a state of war exists between Great Britain and Germany as from 11pm on August 4."

We was all out in the streets – very patriotic, songs and singing and all that. I reckon even the Germans heard us singing 'Rule Britannia'! Some chaps went up outside Buckingham Palace, waiting for the news… you can bet they cheered when they heard it. Now we're off to report for 9am roll call. You up and ready, Fred?

Fred: I'll see you there.

Walter: Here's a photograph of everyone from last night, cheering the announcement.

Walter: What a day! Got paid £5 in gold, plus 10 shillings for having all of me kit. This is better than when I won on the Grand National. They told us to open a Post Office savings account – not likely… that'll be drunk away tonight by most of the lads I reckon.

Fred: I can't even spend mine. Looks like everyone's been at it already so there ain't no change for a sovereign anywhere in Battersea.

Mary: You bring that money back here, Walter, with not a penny missing.

6th August

Walter: They've got grindstones in the drill hall now so everyone's sharpening their bayonets, ready to stick it to old Fritz. Some of the officers brought their swords and sharpened them too. Now it's starting to feel like we're really going to war.

7th August

Walter: We been commandeering horses and wagons today. The grocer weren't too keen to give up his van, even though he signed the form to allow it years ago! We told him it was 'marked for regimental transport' and it was our duty as soldiers to take it off him. He gets paid for the use of it so I don't know what he was grumbling about. Did cause a stir when all the local tradesmen's wagons showed up on the parade ground. Gave us all a laugh.

10th August

Lily: It would be nice to hear from you Walter. Are you getting on alright? I heard there was some trouble with the band.

Fred: Looks like she's got the hump with you!

Walter: I'm sorry, Lily. We been so busy and caught up in it. It didn't go down well with the regimental band that they was supposed to be mobilised too. They didn't think they'd get called up so it was a shock. In the end they got told they don't have to go abroad just yet.

Lily: I didn't think you had to go abroad either?

Fred: Oho! This gets better and better…

| Walter: | Cheese it, Fred. I wasn't sure how to tell you, Lil, but we might get the chance to sign up for going abroad. I'd miss you and all that but I should like to see a different country. |

Walter: Cheese it, Fred. I wasn't sure how to tell you, Lil, but we might get the chance to sign up for going abroad. I'd miss you and all that but I should like to see a different country.

Mary: Just seen this Walter, what do you mean? I've got Charles going off to France with the regular army – you're not going anywhere.

Walter: I've not been training for nothing, Ma! If they need me to fight overseas you can bet I'll be there. Can we talk about this at home later?

11th August

Walter: Had a talk from the CO. He told us all about signing up to say we're willing to go overseas if they need us. Me and Fred was right at the front of the queue. Some fellows thought twice about it once they actually had to sign their name, but not us. In the end only one chap didn't sign the form but I reckon we can sway him.

Army Form E.624.

A G R E E M E N T   to be made by an Officer or man

of the Territorial Force to subject himself to leability

to serve in any place outside the United Kingdom in the

event of national emergency.

I, (No.)..................(Rank).....................

(Name)..... ....(Company)...........

of the (Unit) .... HEREBY

AGREE subject to the conditions stated overleaf, to accept

liability, in the event of national emergency, to serve

in any place outside the United Kingdom, in accordance

with the provisions of Section X111 (2) (a) of the

Territorial and Reserve Forces Act, 1907.

Mary: I'm sorry we couldn't talk you round, son. I know Lily's taken it hard. All the same, as I was saying to Mrs Wiggins today, it does make you proud to have two brave boys going off to fight for King and Country.

12th August

Walter:	Passed the medical, nothing wrong with me! Fred stupidly told them he's got a stiff arm from his portering work and they nearly passed him for home service only, but he said quick he was only joking and they let him through.
Fred:	That was close! Don't know what I was thinking. It's me rifle arm too so they definitely wouldn't have let me sign up.
Lily:	I hope it don't give you trouble when you're out there.
Fred:	Course it won't – won't be doing no portering, will I? Be a chance to give it a rest. Get some sunshine on me and a nice French girl to kiss it better… I'll be right as ninepence in no time.

13th August

Walter:	The billeting party have set us up at St Albans so we're off tomorrow. Parade at headquarters at noon and then we start the march. It's finally time. Can't wait. How do you fancy a walk this evening, Lily? It would be nice to see you.
Lily:	I thought you'd never ask…
Walter:	I ain't planning no big gestures, mind. Just thought it'd be nice to see my girl before I go. I'll knock for you at 6 and we'll go round the block a bit. Maybe up by the bandstand.
Lily:	I'll look forward to it!
Charles:	We're on our way today, Walt, and the people of Dublin gave us a right good send off and a packet of fruit, cake and cigs for each of us!
Walter:	Sounds good, Charlie! Enjoy the trip.
Charles:	Don't know about enjoying it, would you enjoy rattling around in a cattle truck? About to cross the channel – some of the boys are getting a bit nervous. It would be difficult enough without thinking about the German Navy lying in wait for us.

14th August

Fred:	I tell you what, Walter, I'm jiggered. I was half ready to go back to bed when we reached Hyde Park, and then to have to march on to Edgware with all the others!
Lily:	So you're at Edgware now?
Walter:	Yes, Lil – in bivouac at Canons Park. Fred's just pretending, we're having a grand time really. Hyde Park looked wonderful with all the soldiers and their horses. Met a couple of fellows from the 1st Life Guards. More marching tomorrow – all the way up to St Albans.

15th August

Walter: Marched the rest of the way to St Albans today. Arrived like heroes as the band played us all the way up the hill into the town. Felt quite proud. Billeted at a nice place on the west of the city but some of the rest are up on the north side. I feel for Fred – he's only up the road but he must be in the most narrowest house I ever saw. Bad luck, Fred!

Fred: It ain't so bad. Living with a nice old fellow – he made me cocoa and everything. He don't have no family here so I think it suits him just fine.

Mary: Who are you billeted with, Walter? I hope they treat you alright.

Walter: Haven't met all of them yet, Ma – it's a family with a couple of kids and their nan living with them. A Mr and Mrs Abbott. They seem alright. I'm here with another fellow from our battalion, Bert Hopkins. I suppose they wanted the extra money for taking two of us. Bert says you know his mum. We're sharing a room like I do with Ed at home. Hope he's a better bedfellow that you, Eddie…

| Ed: | Well I'm stretching out here now… very nice to have a room all to meself! |
| Mary: | I do know her – I'll have a word next time I see her down the butcher's. Sleep well son. |

15th August

| Walter: | How are you getting on, Charlie? |
| Charles: | Landed in France, at Le Havre – soaking rain though so can't see much. Will set off 'on root' (how's that for some French!) to Belgium on Monday. |

| Walter: | Good luck. Wish I was there with you as I reckon it'll be all over by the time we get there. Give Fritz a bellyful from me if you see him. |

17th August

Walter:	Starting to know me way around now – they've set up battalion headquarters, sergeants' mess and central messing at the Abbey and County Hall, and we've got a good bit of Batchwood Park for training. Met the rest of the family too – Jimmy and Jack, the little'uns, are a laugh. Jimmy's at school – he says he's nearly 9 and almost old enough to be a soldier hisself. Ha. Little Jack's only 3 so he's still at home with his Ma. Then there's Mrs Abbott's Old Nana, who I have to call 'Miss Sarah', but who everyone on the street calls 'Ol' Great Western' because she always tells how she "came hootin' into the world the same time as the trains, dear." She told me this a few times already.
Lily:	Seems like you're settling in and they sound a nice bunch. Just don't go meeting no glamorous ladies.
Walter:	Oh it ain't glamorous here at all, Lil. Quite like the countryside compared to London. Must say I like it though. Quiet enough. And anyway, we spend all our time training – no time to meet no ladies.

19th August

| Walter: | Heard something funny from little Jimmy today. He said his mate was on scout camp when war was declared, with a German scoutmaster! The fellow left immediately, but Mrs Abbott says he only got as far as Dover and they must have taken him to prison. Good job too. Reckon them Germans have got spies everywhere. |

21st August

| Walter: | Any updates, Charlie? |

| Charles: | Quick one while I've got a moment to write to you. Left our billets at Landrecies at 6.30 this morning for more marching… 15 miles past the Forest of Mormal. Weather very close and muggy. Lots of reservists joined us before we left – glad of them as we were low on men but it's strange to suddenly get new chaps when you know the usual ones so well. They're finding it very trying. I'm alright. Haven't even seen a German yet and already got one casualty – Walters was bathing in the canal and was drowned. Bit of a shock. Poor fellow's going to miss the whole thing. |

| Mary: | Thanks for this son and I'm sorry to hear about your friend. Give us all the news whenever you can. |

| Walter: | Poor chap. Glad to hear you're getting on alright, Charlie. |

22nd August

| Charles: | More marching up to the Mons Conde Canal today. 18 miles. Very hot. Every road in Belgium seems cobbled and it ain't half hard on the feet. Worse for the reservists with their new boots – they've worked hard to get fit but the boots take weeks to break in. I ain't seen it meself but they say they have blood coming through their lace holes! They can't even have a foot inspection because they're all afraid if they take the boots off they might not get them back on again… and now we're here we ain't got no supplies and was told to eat half our iron ration already. |

| Walter: | Poor chaps! Glad I've had me boots a while… Hope you had a cup of tea at least, Charlie. Have you see any Germans yet? |

| Charles: | Not yet, but we had reports of a couple of cavalry skirmishes. All we can do is strengthen our positions here, to the left of the French. The canal's important as we need to stop Fritz getting beyond it and heading for Paris. There are two bridges here near Les Herbieres, out to the west of Mons – a railway bridge and a road bridge. Ours to guard, with the 2nd Kings Own Scottish Borderers. |

| Walter: | I wish I was there Charlie… it sounds so exciting to be up there with the boys doing some good. Feel a bit cut off here in St Albans. |

23rd August

Walter:	Charlie, I heard there's been some enemy action up there. Hope you gave him what for. Let us know how you're getting on when you can.
Mary:	We're fretting here – Annie keeps asking how her biggest brother is and I can't tell her.
Walter:	I'm sure he'll be fine, Ma. Tell Annie that Charlie's the strongest fellow there. He won't let no German come near him. He's probably too busy fighting them off one-handed to write, that's all.

24th August

Walter:	Charlie?
Charles:	2am – just got to bed, bivouacked in a factory yard to the south. Exhausted. 100 of our battalion are dead, wounded or missing, maybe more. Chalky's gone, Pearce, Eddie. He were only a foot away from me and they got him. I'm sorry you had to wait for news. Tell Annie I'm alright, Ma.
Walter:	What happened? So sorry about your pals.
Charles:	The Hun attacked at 1pm. Artillery bombardment first, then Fritz himself. There's so many of them, Walt. More than us. They came forward in a block but was just walking, so we gave them some – our riflemen are the best there are and you can't beat the Mk III SMLE for accuracy. You couldn't miss them anyway, them coming forward like that. Don't know how many I got. Lots. The machine gunners held them off at the bridges too but there was too many of them and they broke through the Borderers' barricade. . . we had to withdraw south. Only a bit though. And the Royal Engineers blew up the bridges so Fritz couldn't get over.
Walter:	Sounds like you gave him a rough time. Well done Charlie. Glad you're alright.
Charlie:	We're holding him back. Have to sleep now – only got a couple of hours.

24th August

Charles:	3.50am – up again. Parading at 4am. Very tired. There's rumours that the French are retreating. Stupid if you ask me – the BEF could stick it, but not if the French leave a gap to our side. Could get surrounded so we'll have to pull back if they do.
Walter:	Not what anyone was expecting – I thought you was going to blast straight through him? There's nothing about any of this in the papers.
Charles:	I told you, there's too many. We'll keep him off Paris but we'll have to retreat for a bit. Just been told I'm on rear guard now while we pull back. Going to be a long, hot march.
Walter:	Good luck.

26th August

Walter:	How is it, Charlie?
Charles:	Very tiring. I'd say we've lost more men in this retreat than we did in the battle. Arrived at Le Cateau last night but a lot of fuss to get there. Our whole army was split in two to march either side of the forest. Meant to be quicker that way or something, and we have to be quick – the Hun are on our backs night and day. Got reinforcements now – chaps from the 3rd Division. We were meant to fall back to St Quentin, where GHQ has retreated to, but Fritz was coming up too close and General Smith Dorrien said we had to stay and make a stand against him here at Le Cateau. We was all so glad to finally turn around and fight, but it weren't pretty, Walt. We thought I Corps would come to back us up but they never did. Battlefield a bit like Salisbury Plain without the trees – nowhere to hide and the Germans all on high ground to the north. Got buried by a shell blast… but got meself out again. Out of all the line they say us in the 5th Division in the west got it worst, but the right flank got wiped out too. Saw a lot of good mates go down. Not going to list them no more, there's too many. Don't worry, though Walt, we're holding him back.
Walter:	That don't sound good. How did you get away?
Charles:	In the end the Yorkshire infantrymen covered us while we retreated south. I'll be honest, there ain't many of us left. They say we started out with 80,000 men and the Germans with 750,000. In the east it's 250,000 Germans versus 800,000 Russians. Don't know what our numbers are now. Don't like to think. We stopped them at Le Cateau for a while though. Gives us a chance to get further south. Heading for St Quentin – marching overnight. 25 miles.

27th August

Walter: Thought of you today, Charlie – Mrs Abbott was asking me all about me brothers and sisters. Proud of you, brother. How are you getting on? There's still nothing about the retreat in the papers…

Charles: Thanks Walt. Paraded at 3am and marched to St Quentin. Bit quieter here, but the Hun are never far behind. Some fellows from 4th Division was going to surrender, owing to not wanting to march no more… but they say Major Tom Bridges and his trumpeter walked into a toy shop, bought a toy drum and a tin whistle and did a speech with music to stir them up again! Ha. I could do with some stirring up meself. How are you getting on in St Albans? Tell me all the news, it'll give me something to take me mind off the hunger. I shall be glad to get to somewhere where we can get proper supplies and some cooked food.

Walter: Great story. Hope you get some hot food soon. We're getting on alright – always marching here too. Sounds like we're going to need the practice, from what you said. We ain't had any bayonet assault training at all though – suppose we might not need it with all the rifle and artillery action!

Charles: Don't be soft. You'll always need your bayonet – it's great for toasting bread, opening cans, scraping mud off your boots…

29th August

Walter: I had a letter from Ma, Rose… says she ain't happy with you and to have a word. What is it now?

Rose: I told her I'm signing up to go to France… You remember when I joined the Civil Hospital Reserve so I could be a military nurse in wartime, but still have me civilian nursing job when I came back? Well, I didn't tell you… but, like you, I had the chance to sign up to go abroad instead of just staying here. You can bet I did it. Me and Edie from the Lodging House went together. Ma ain't happy though – she says with Charles there and you going she won't have any of her eldest children left, except Ed…

Walter: Right, first off, Ma – I probably ain't even going. Charlie's lot will have finished him off before we even leave. Secondly, Rose – you ain't got your head on straight. France can do without one more nurse. It ain't the place for you. You heard what Charlie said, it's dangerous enough even for the men.

Rose: Well ain't you all high and mighty now you're out of the house! Yes, I saw what Charlie wrote. That's just it – I can't have me big brother and our boys out there and not do nothing to help. The military nurses ain't enough and they need us reserves.

Ed: I don't see why you'd bother, Rose. Stay here where it's safe.

Mary: I don't know what to do with her. I've told her she'll have to have her father's permission before she can go, not that that's ever stopped her. If you'd been married by now Rose, you wouldn't be giving your mother so much grief.

Rose: How many times, Ma… I can't do nursing proper if I'm married, and they wouldn't have let me sign up to go to France anyway. Besides, I like living with the girls in the Lodging House.

Charles: Just got a quiet minute to reply sorry everyone, but we need more nurses like you Rosie. It ain't a place for women out here, especially not me little sister, but that don't mean we don't need you. Just you mind them jack-the-lads… tell them you're engaged or something.

Walter: Well, if Charlie says… when do you think you might go out?

Rose: As soon as I can – October maybe. Thanks, Charlie, hope you're alright.

Charles: Alright here, got a bit of cooked food yesterday morning (usually we just pick cold stuff up from 'dumps' they leave for us at the side of the road…) then it was more marching, but we've been able to rest at Pontpoise today.

Mary: Take good care, son. We're very proud of you Rose, you come and speak to your father.

30th August

Charles: Bad news from the Eastern Front. The Russians have been trying to give us lot a break by attacking the Germans from the east, but it ain't gone well. Yesterday, three whole corps of the Russian army got surrounded in a forest with no way out. They say the enemy took 92,000 prisoners and killed tens of thousands more.

31st August

Charles: Rotten day. As one of the officers said – "Exceedingly hot, what?" That's become our little saying now. I does quite a good impression when he ain't listening. Couldn't stop for our noonday halt, owing to reports of Germans coming up too close, so we had to keep marching in the heat and some of the men 'fell out' towards the end. Got more men yesterday though – there weren't many of the 2nd Suffolk Regiment left so they've been added to us.

Walter: Sounds like you're one of the fittest there, Charlie. Can't wait to come and join you.

September 1914

———◆———

3rd September

Charles:	Moved at 4am to Montge, now have very comfortable billets in a French chateau! Can see the outskirts of Paris from the window. Strange to think that's what we're trying to protect.
Walter:	Didn't realise you were so close. I always wanted to see the Eiffel Tower. Maybe I'll take you there one day Lily.

Lily:	That would be nice. Except I don't like heights…
Walter:	I reckon you'd be alright with me. Just you keep the Tower standing Charlie, then me and Lil can go up it next year when the war's over!
Charles:	If all goes well I shan't even be going near it.

5th September

Charles:	You should see us now, Walter – still on the march but with a squadron of North Irish Horse helping by day and a platoon of cyclists by night! Still "exceedingly hot, what" and I'd just about curse whoever thought it was a good idea to give us these heavy uniforms, not to mention everything else we has to carry. Moving down to the east of Paris now. Seems to have been a change of plan. All hoping we might get to stop this retreat and lay into Fritz before he gets any further.
Charles:	Bit of news – looks like the enemy ain't headed for Paris now and just wants to wipe out the French army. Getting the information from aeroplanes! New one on me.

6th September

Charles:	Reveille at 3.45am. Couldn't sleep anyway. Today's the day – we've finally been given the go-ahead to change direction and go on the offensive. One officer said it's the happiest day of his life.
Walter:	Good luck, Charlie.
Mary:	We're always thinking about you, son. Good luck.

7th September

Walter:	How are you going on Charlie?
Charles:	Nothing doing yet – having to stand by. Want to get going. Marching east when we can. A Captain Whish and about 100 other men have joined us. Word is the French have had lots of casualties so the reserves have been called in – they were taken to the front in taxis from Paris! Renaults it was. About 3,000 men. Must have been a sight.

8th September

Charles:	What a joke of a day. Fought hard through the thick wood around Chateau-St-Ouen – full of steep banks and streams, even had to take a small boat (one little boat for two battalions…). Then the CO got some information about exactly where Fritz was hiding – he'd dug trenches on the opposite ridge of the valley. So we came around to the right, to hit him on his flank. All had our bayonets out, excited to finally get a chance to stick it to the enemy, man-to-man, like the CO promised. A few casualties as we advanced but we was going on well and the enemy was retreating, when all of a sudden our Artillery opened fire all along the ridge. Right over our heads – sounded like being under a railway bridge. The CO tried to get them to stop but it was no good. We had to fall back behind the line of fire. After all that. Took a couple of prisoners during the day but still right disappointed. Captain Whish died – that chap that joined us yesterday.
Walter:	Rotten luck, Charlie. Glad you're alright. Still no chance to use our bayonets here in St Albans neither. Are you back at camp now?
Charles:	Back where we bivouacked earlier… not much to show for it, except when we got back we found some of our men who had been cut off from us in August. Turns out after the fighting they found themselves closest to 1st Division so joined up with them. When they left though, 1st Division kept their horses and vehicles!

| Walter: | They've got a nerve. |

9th September

| Walter: | Any news from the Front? |

| Charles: | Busy day. Moved at 5am towards the Marne river. We were the Advanced Guard (the brigades take it in turns to take different positions when we're on the move – Sarge says it's like penguins trying to keep warm). Very trying as lots of thick woods and steep valleys. Heavy artillery fire from the Boche. Tried to keep meself hidden under the trees. Was sent towards the German trenches. Hail of bullets. Fell back. Went in again with reinforcements. Hail of bullets. Fell back again. Went in again with more reinforcements. Hail of bullets. Fell back again. Couldn't believe I'd made it out. Got a bit knocked about and took a bullet across me arm – only a scratch but you've got to go careful in case of gangrene. Treated by the Medical Officer at the Regimental Aid Post and then straight back out again. Fritz was still in his trench at nightfall but we must've put the wind up him because he ran off soon after. Word is we're getting in between the German 1st and 2nd Armies, and soon enough he'll be on the run for good. |

| Walter: | Told you, Ma! We Carters, we're made of strong stuff! Tell Annie that Charlie was the only fellow to make it out and he chased them Germans off all by hisself. Won't be nothing left for us to do if we ever get out there, eh Fred? |

| Fred: | Can't believe it, just when I got me rifle eye in as well. At least I won't have to get on a boat. |

| Mary: | Annie's asking what happened to his friends then and is he lonely… poor little love doesn't really understand. |

| Charles: | I'm starting to think it won't be over so quick, Walt – best keep preparing. Little Annie's a clever old stick… tell her it do get lonely, but only because I miss her. |

11th September

Charles: Well at least it ain't hot no more. Trouble is, it's pouring rain and we can hardly get along the tracks. Rough time yesterday – a party of us was left behind to bury the dead that was laid along the side of the road. Not easy, especially with me bad arm. Hope we got them deep enough – we didn't have much time. We had the chaplain with us and tried to give them a proper burial and that but it's hard when you're moving on. Still pushing the Germans back towards the North of France. Crossing the River Aisne soon. Got to make a raft.

13th September

Walter: Word is we get to leave St Albans for a while for musketry camp. I'll miss little Jimmy and Jack but it won't be for long. Perfect conditions at the moment so should go off well. Will be at Panshanger near Hertingfordbury – I'll send you a temporary address to write to, Lil.

Lily: Thanks. I know you're busy but I like to hear from you.

Walter: What's happening back in Battersea? Hope you're all getting on alright without us!

Lily: We're just fine, thank you kindly… but it's quiet without our boys around. There's still quite a few, like your Ed, who haven't volunteered, but people are starting to say that women could step up and take the men's jobs what have gone! How do you think I'd do as a porter eh, Walt?

Walter: Ha! I can just see you in me uniform, lugging cases about! Ha ha. Don't be daft though, you've got your job.

15th September

Walter: I've been thinking about what Lil was saying, Ed, and I don't know what you're playing at, not volunteering. You must have seen the posters of Kitchener – they're everywhere. I read that they asked for 100,000 volunteers and 750,000 joined up in just one month. That's British pluck that is. Find yourself a backbone.

Ed: If they only needed 100,000, and 750,000 signed up, then what do they need me for? Don't make no sense to put meself in danger for some Austrian problem I don't even understand. You're the ones need your heads looking at.

Walter: Don't understand, he says… we was protecting Belgium. They're neutral, they're staying out of it, but Germany didn't take no notice and went right through them to get to France… Why don't you join a Pals battalion? Then you could go with your mates.

SAD EXPERIENCES OF BIG AND LITTLE WILLIE.—No. 8.

Mary: If your father could hear you, Edward. I'm frightened to send my boys away but the shame of having a shirker stay behind is too much. How your brothers grew up with such grit and you didn't, I'll never know. Even Rose wants to go out there, God save her. Too much chasing girls, that's what did it. Well you'll find that those young ladies ain't so keen on you now, not when they could go with a soldier.

Ed: Minnie says she thinks I'm braver not going.

Rose: Who's Minnie? I thought it was Eliza?

Ed: It was, but now it ain't. Minnie's a nice girl, you'd like her.

Mary: One of these days I'll wash my hands of you, Edward Carter.

Walter: Here are the brave chaps signing up, Ed.

16th September

Walter: Ed, you ought to get yourself to see a Vesta Tilley show – she recruits men for the army right there in the music hall and gives you kiss if you sign up…!

Ed: She can have her show, I ain't going.

Fred: Well, I wish I'd waited and volunteered now – don't fancy a kiss off none of you Terriers!

17th September

Walter: How are you getting on, Charlie?

Charles: Rain and digging, Walt. And then more rain and digging. Rain don't half make digging hard.

Walter: What are you digging for?

Charles: Trenches – ain't you practised that yet? We has to protect ourselves from the bullets somehow and it helps if you can shelter a bit below ground. They ain't fancy ones, we've just dug them quick to cover us for the next day or so. The Germans have already dug trenches on the high ground and we can't get past them, so we're stuck with the wet low ground and have to dig too. All the digging has to be done at night, mind, so they can't see us so easy.

Walter: We're going to practise digging trenches in Essex when we've done the musketry – we'll be back in St Albans in a couple of days. You lot out in France have got all the sandbags though, so we can't do it proper.

Charles: We ain't just digging trenches, mind – it's graves too. You wouldn't believe it, but we been burying dead Germans as well as our boys – the ones what gets left behind when we advance on them. There's something about seeing the results of your work that makes a man think.

19th September

Walter:	I heard the suffragettes have finally given up… is that right, Lil?
Lily:	Well, they ain't given up exactly… it's just Mrs Pankhurst says we has to do everything we can for the war effort and then think about the vote again afterwards. Her daughter Christabel made a speech about it. She reckons the French women are all working while the men are at the Front and that we should do the same. This is what she said, look: "You are not now utilising to the full the activities of women. In France, from which country I have just come, the women, while all the able-bodied men are at the Front, are able to keep the country going, to get in the harvest, to carry on the industries. It is the women who prevent the collapse of the nation while the men are fighting the enemy."

21st September

Charles:	I never thought I'd get used to the sound of whizz-bangs but today, for once, we had a quiet morning and it seemed eerie. Didn't last long though as Fritz started shelling the village in the early afternoon. We been here at Missy-sur-Aisne for a few days now so it was sad to see the buildings get knocked about. Bit worried about a little friend I made – Marie. We'll be moving on anyway but I shouldn't like anything to happen to her.
Walter:	Now there's the one thing you'd sign up for, Ed the lovely ladies of France! Glad you're alright Charlie.
Charles:	Course I'm alright. The Sergeant Major and CO had a close run though – they was walking into the hospital to see some of our boys when a shell fell right in between them… both made it out but the stretcher bearer copped a packet. Nothing like the number of men we usually lose, mind.

Walter: Glad you're alright – shame about the stretcher bearer. There was a new poem in The Times today that said, "They shall grow not old, as we that are left grow old: Age shall not weary them, nor the years condemn. At the going down of the sun and in the morning We will remember them." Bit bleedin, sad, ain't it?

24th September

Walter: Happy birthday to my Ma! Sorry I'm up here in St Albans and not with you but have a nice day.

Charles: Hope I'll be home for the next one – happy birthday!

Rose: Happy birthday, Ma. I'll be round as usual in the morning.

Mary: Thank you very much. It's been a quiet birthday, and not much good news – Maud from up the road got a form saying Billy is missing. We can't console her. The note says he might be a Prisoner of War – I hope so.

Charles: That is bad news – poor old Bill. Hope they find him – sometimes men get separated from their regiment for a while so he might find his way back.

25th September

Charles: What a good day we've had. The Dorsets relieved us back at Missy so we marched along the railway line at 4am this morning and now have billets at Jury. Time for a rest. Commander Smith-Dorrien came by our billets hisself and said how proud we must be and how well we done. Not only that but we been reclothing. Feels better than you'd ever think to have a fresh, clean uniform – seems like I been wearing nothing but mud for weeks.

Mary: Well done, son, we're all very proud of you.

Walter: That's great Charlie. Have a good rest. Did you see Marie?

Charles: No. Don't know what happened to her. That's how it goes out here. Shouldn't say too much about it anyway, we ain't supposed to talk to them – although word is we might get a little book of French words soon.

27th September

Charles: Got woke up at 3am because of a rumour that the Germans was coming up close. They wasn't, but we'd got a fair way away before we found that out. Had a Divine Service for the whole battalion in a field when we got back. Only a few fellows didn't turn up. Quiet time is a bit difficult when you start to think about everything what's happened, but the padre says God is on our side. My pal Hibbs says one of the Germans he knocked out had 'Gott mit uns' (reckons it means 'God with us') written on his belt though, so who knows what the old fellow's playing at.

30th September

Lily: Walt, you're not going to like this but I thought I ought to let you know… There's a fellow called Herbert who comes in Arding & Hobbs a lot. Mabel always laughs and says he's taken a liking to me, but I didn't think nothing of it until he come in today with a great bunch of lavender roses (well you know they're my favourite) and made a big show about how pretty I was and how I deserved a fellow who was around to take care of me. Well I went red as a beetroot – it ain't like I've been acting like I'm available, Walt… You'll be pleased to know I told him I didn't need no looking after and besides, I deserve a fellow who's brave enough to fight for King and Country – said I noticed he weren't wearing khaki. He said he were all for love, not war, and tried to give me the roses again! Well I kept them in the end because they were nice, but I made sure he knew I was waiting for my Walter. The girls did have a laugh about it though and Mrs Reed sent me home for causing a scene! I think secretly she was glad that I said he ought to be out fighting because she says I can go back tomorrow.

Walter: Too right I don't like it! I don't mind telling you that's given me the right hump, Lil. And a shirker as well! He's got a nerve. I've a mind to come straight down there and knock the living daylights out of him. Are you sure you're alright? He didn't hurt you or nothing?

Lily: Of course he didn't hurt me, silly!

Walter: Well, good. You just make sure everyone knows you're spoken for. Pretty thing like you, it's no good you being down there by yourself… it's just that I can't get back while I have to be training. Maybe I could send you some little token or something, just so all the 'Herberts' know you're mine.

Lily: A ring would do it…

Walter: Well now hold on I don't mean nothing like that. I meant a badge or a locket or something.

October 1914

1st October

Rose: Get ready for a shock everyone – I'm on me way to France! Going out with a group of reinforcements to join our old Matron at one of the Base Hospitals. Couldn't tell you before I left because I didn't want no one getting upset. I'm alright though, quite enjoying meself so far, even if the boat has to have all its lights out in case we're seen. Feels quite eerie. I never even been on a boat before.

Walter: You've got a nerve, Rose! I dread to think what Ma will say…

Mary: You silly, silly girl. And to not even see us before you left… it breaks my heart. Your father left the house without a word when I told him – just slammed the door. Well, you're on your own now – don't go crying to me when you want to come home.

Rose: I don't want to come home, I want to be out there helping! I'm tougher than you think – you don't know the half of what I've seen in them hospitals back home. And boys like our Charlie need us, so there it is. And I'm sorry I didn't come to see you – I reckon I was afraid if I did you'd talk me out of it.

Walter:	She's a brave girl, Ma, you have to give her that.
Mary:	She might be brave, but I'm scared stiff. I expect we would have talked you out of it too, but it's only because we love you, Rosie. And I don't doubt you've seen plenty at the Workhouse Infirmary, but it ain't war.
Rose:	I know, but I'm here to learn ain't I? I'll write to you as often as I can, let you know I'm alright. Who knows, I might even see Charlie!
Charles:	We've just been given the order to march north so you might! Hopefully with all me limbs in one place though. Where will you be?
Rose:	Boulogne, I think. That's where the boat's headed. I'll let you know.

6th October

Walter:	You'd have been proud of me today, Lily – we was inspected by Field Marshal Earl Roberts hisself! The whole battalion in the grounds of St Albans County Hall. He said we was very smart and gave us a speech about fighting for our country. All of us wanted to get straight on a boat and get out there after that. Hope the call comes soon – we been doing that much marching, I'm sure we're as fit as we'll ever be. You make sure you tell that Herbert fellow when you see him, Lil. In fact, don't see him.

Lily:	I'll bet you looked handsome. I miss you so much. Don't worry about Herbert, he ain't been back. Your Ma said maybe I could go with her and Ed to visit you soon – what do you think? It'd be too much for little Annie so she's going to stop with Mrs Hibbs.
Walter:	Well, that's the best news I've had all week! You'll be alright if you come up with them. Won't get much chance to be by ourselves though.
Lily:	I suppose we'll see what we can manage.
Mary:	Don't think I won't be watching you like me own daughter, Lily Howes. I reckon everywhere should have a sign like at them Lodging Houses where Rose was – 'KEEP INNOCENCY'.

8th October

Walter:	Well, what's it like out there, Rosie?

Rose: Hello everyone – first chance I've had to write, we been so busy. What a place Boulogne is… all the hotels (with their posh 'chandeliers' and everything) have been turned into hospitals and there's wounded soldiers and makeshift ambulances everywhere. Some of the poor fellows are in a bad way. They can't always get them off the battlefield first thing so they come to us after days of lying out in the rain and mud. The first few days was the worst – I seen some things that would make you shudder and a fair few that would make you blush. First thing I saw when I come through the door was a chap having his dressings changed – a piece of shrapnel had torn his cheek right off – you could see his whole jawbone. They was trying to keep the wound clean. I ain't never heard a man scream like that. You were right, Ma, it ain't like the Infirmary. Got to make the best of it though… and I'm glad of my training.

Lily: Sounds like you're doing a great job, Rose. What a thing to do. Let us know how you get on.

Walter: Well done, sis. Get them back out there as quick as you can.

10th October

Walter: You alright, John? Heard you went out to Antwerp. Sounds like it's been tough going.

John: Tough ain't the word. Some of us Naval Reserve got made into a couple of brigades for fighting on land – the idea was to go and help the Belgians defend Antwerp against the Germans. When we got there though, the Belgian government had already left and they wanted to evacuate the people too. We thought we could stick it but the German artillery was just too much, we didn't have nothing as big as that to fire back with and they broke through the walls around the city. Well, as soon as it was clear how much damage they could do with them heavy howitzers the people started evacuating, and Antwerp surrendered today. Not surprising – they didn't even have any water there (not for drinking or putting out fires) after the waterworks got destroyed. At least we held Fritz there a few days while the rest of the Allies blocked the coastal routes. Don't want the enemy getting near Calais. Some of our lot have escaped over to the Netherlands, which is keeping neutral. The rest of us are on our way back to England already. Due in at Charing Cross tomorrow. It has been a rotten few days. I'm glad to be out of it – get me back on a ship.

at Antwerp, just before our
visit to the trenches.

11th October

Walter: Little Jimmy asked if you'd seen any foreigners, Charlie? I told him you'd seen a lot of Germans – live ones and dead ones. He liked that… but he said what about the French men or any Russian ones – what are they like?

Charles: You can tell him dead Germans is just like dead Englishmen with different hats on. We all looks the same blown to bits. The French, well they've got blue uniforms and moustaches and say "toot sweet" when they want you to hurry up. Some of the boys reckon they've got North African troops with them too. Not seen them yet. Seen a lot of Belgians coming down from the north – refugees who had to leave their villages when Fritz came calling. Some of them has horses and wagons but there's lots just walking, carrying whatever they could get tied up in sheets. Some of the men have got guns, some just umbrellas. Not much use as a bayonet they'd be. I ain't seen no Russians or Austrians – they're fighting off on the Eastern Front.

13th October

Charles:	Moving north at a good old pace towards Ypres now (good luck pronouncing that – we just calls it 'Wipers') and the rest days at Jury feel like a long time ago. The whole army is always trying to get around the top side of the enemy to hem him in (we pivot to the right – takes a while), but it seems Fritz has the same idea. Sometimes I reckon we're all just fighting our way to the sea. Don't know what'll happen when we hit it…
Walter:	Any action lately?
Charles:	Every day little brother, and sometimes the night too. Fighting with their rear guard, so at least that means we're pushing him back. Fought over farms and farmland today. Looked like whoever lived there had already left – probably one of them refugee families we passed. Sometimes I think about how much of their harvest has got ruined under our feet, with the shells and the digging and all that. Poor chaps probably didn't even want a war in the first place.

14th October

Walter:	I been thinking about your run-in with that Herbert chap, Lil, and I got something for you. It's a cap badge from our battalion. You could put it on your blouse or something. I've seen some of the girls up here doing it, just so you know they're thinking of a fellow somewhere. Will you wear it for me?
Lily:	Oh Walt, that's nice of you! Yes I'll wear it, of course I will. Some of the other girls in the shop have them and they ain't half proud. Herb came back in yesterday – says as long as I'll wait for you, he'll wait for me that long plus a day. He do know how to turn on the charm, I'll give him that. I sent him packing again though, don't worry.
Walter:	I should hope you did. And charm don't count for nothing anyway – he ain't protecting his country, is he? I'll get this to you in the post as quick as I can, and you just remember it every time some other fellow thinks he can get a look in.

16th October

Charles: Heavy fog today (just like them pea soupers back in London, Ma!). Advanced at 5.30 this morning. A couple of the newer fellows got wounded. Gets difficult sometimes when you're lumbered with men who've just come out... but there ain't many of us regulars left so we has to have reinforcements. The Germans are getting crafty with their gunfire too – yesterday they put a maxim machine gun on top of a motor car and drove it up and down behind their line, firing at us.

Mary: That sounds terrible... I do worry about you. Thinking about pea soupers – do you remember that time I thought I'd lost you in the fog on St John's Hill when you was little? Horrid that was. Bless your heart, when I found you, you said, "I been standing still Ma, like you told me". Dear little one. Thinking of you out there in the fog makes me want to bundle you up and bring you home.

Charles: Thank heavens the boys out here can't hear you, I'd never hear the end of it! "I been standing still, like you told me..." Ha ha. No standing still here while the enemy is on the move anyway. We're holding them back, Ma – if we let them get through Ypres they'll be at the ports in no time and over to Dover. We'll fight to the last man so that don't happen.

18th October

Walter: Did you get the badge I sent you, Lil?

Lily: Just this morning! Thanks. It is nice. I'll have a look and see where I can put it.

Walter: Put it where everyone can see it, I say. Pin it to your blouse, where Herbert can't miss it.

20th October

Lily: We're going to come and see you at the weekend, Walt! How about that? It'll be the 24th...you know what day that is.

Walter: Great news! I can't wait to see you. The 24th of October though... nope, that don't ring no bells...

Lily:	You're rotten, Walter Carter! You know very well it's my birthday!
Walter:	Ha ha, you can see right through me. I'd love to see you for your birthday sweetheart – 19 years old and prettier every day, I reckon. Got a bit of training on Saturday but not all day. Can't wait for you to meet the Abbotts and all the lads. The Terrier boys are a bit rough but don't take no notice.
Lily:	I won't mind them, you know that – I think they're a laugh. How's Charlie getting on in France?
Walter:	He's doing a grand job, Lil – they've lost a lot of men but our Charlie's got some sort of charm on him. Them Germans ain't going nowhere with Charles Carter out there holding them back. Ain't that right. Charlie?

21st October

Walter:	Seeing a lot about remembering the Battle of Trafalgar today – more than 100 years ago! 1805… Grateful to the men who gave their lives back then.

TRAFALGAR-DAY.

TO-NIGHT'S TRIBUTE TO THE ALLIED FLEETS.

To-day the nation celebrates the victory of Trafalgar, which protected this country from invasion and secured for Britain the supremacy of the seas.

The flags of the Allies will be hoisted on the public buildings of 261 cities and towns, and this evening a great meeting to pay a tribute to the allied fleets will be held in the London Opera House. Lord Charles Beresford will speak, and those present will include a special delegation from the French Embassy, the Japanese and Russian Ambassadors, the Greek Minister, and the mayors of seventeen London boroughs.

Thousands of people passed yesterday round the decorated Nelson Column in Trafalgar-square, which bore many wreaths in memory of officers and men of the ships lost during the present war. Inscriptions on the wreaths included the following:—

In loving memory of Lieutenant B. J. Carter, who lost his life in H.M.S. Pathfinder. From his mother.

In memory of Lieutenant Gerald Leather, a loved one, who laid down his life for King and country in the Pathfinder.

In loving memory of my dear husband. From his wife and little darling, Minnie and Violet Clarke.

In loving memory of Cadet Bertie Riley.

In proud memory of Lieut.-Commander N. K. W. Barttelot, H.M.S. Liberty, killed in the action off Heligoland.

In loving memory of my dear sweetheart, asleep in the North Sea.

There are nine wreaths from sons and daughters of officers who fought at Trafalgar.

22nd October

Walter:	Have you heard anything from Charlie, Ma?
Mary:	Not a peep. The papers say they've had some trouble up near Ypres – I couldn't sleep last night thinking about it.
Walter:	He'll be alright, anyway… it's Charlie, you know what he's like – he probably ain't had a chance to write if they been busy out there.
Mary:	I hope you're right, son. I gets meself all worked up every time someone comes by the front door – I always think they're bringing bad news. Annie asked me what was wrong so I just told her I'd been chopping the onions for her dinner. She didn't believe me. I'm glad we get to see you at the weekend.

23rd October

Walter: Can't wait to see you and everyone tomorrow, Lil! Still ain't heard from Charlie though… I'm worried about him.

Lily: I know, sweetheart – I'm worried too. I'm sure he'll be in touch soon though, probably just ain't had time to write. I'm so looking forward to seeing you – the only thing is, your Ma might want to stay here to wait for any post about Charlie.

Walter: Yes, she might. I wouldn't want to miss a letter neither. No reason to think you can't come up yourself though… You have to come now anyway as I've told all the lads. They'll think you've stood me up.

Lily: Oh don't be daft, it's just I couldn't come without your Ma. Hope you hear from him soon.

24th October

Walter: I ain't good at writing things like this. Don't even know how to start. It's Charlie. My big brother Charlie. They got him. 'Killed in action' they call it. Near Ypres. He's been gone since Monday and we didn't even know. No details yet, so please don't ask – Ma just got one of them awful forms. He was always so brave and strong and didn't let nothing worry him… I don't think no one thought this would ever happen. I keep thinking about things like when he taught me to ride his bike what was too big for me but he let me have it anyway. It ain't fair for them to take someone good like that. I don't know what we're going to do without him. One thing's for sure, Fritz has got it coming when I get out there. No one takes Charlie from me and gets away with it. I'm going to go and finish the job for him.

Lily: Oh darling. I'm so sorry. I'm so, so sorry. He was such a wonderful man. Shall I come up to be with you? I could get the train.

Walter: Thanks, Lil. No it's alright, I think I can get some leave to come down. I'll be there as soon as I can – need to see you. And Ma. The Abbotts are being very nice, looking after me and being very concerned, but it ain't home.

Lily: Alright love. Glad you're being looked after. It would be good to see you though. I could go to Sabine Road – do you think your Ma would want me round?

Walter: Thank you. I think she'd like to see you, what with Rose being away. If you could help to look after Annie, perhaps.

Lily: I'll go over there now. Your poor Ma, I can't imagine it… Be strong sweetheart and I'll see you soon.

John: Very sorry to hear about your brother, Walter. So many people have had bad news. It ain't right.

Mabel: Oh Walt, and Ed and Rose and all of you – I'm so sorry. Let me know if there's anything I can do – I ain't far away.

Fred: I'll look after him until he gets to you Lil.

Margaret:	Such dreadful news for you all. In times of strife, you must remember that he died fighting for King and Country, which is the greatest honour.

24th October

Walter:	This is the form they sent to Ma about Charlie. Everyone dreads them. She said she heard the knock at the door and didn't think her legs would move to go and answer it.

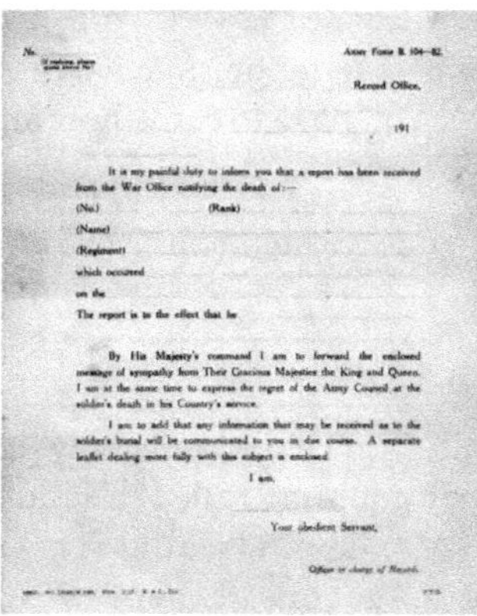

It is my painful duty to inform you that a report has been received from the War Office notifying the death of: -

(No.)......(Rank).......
(Name).......
(Regiment)....
which occurred.....
on the......
The report is to the effect that he......

By His Majesty's command I am to forward the enclosed message of sympathy from Their Gracious Majesties the King and Queen. I am at the same time to express the regret of the Army Council at the soldier's death in his Country's service.

I am to add that any information that may be received as to the soldier's burial will be communicated to you in due course. A separate leaflet dealing more fully with this subject is enclosed.

I am....... Your obedient Servant.

Officer in charge of Records

Walter:	Oh, and happy birthday dearest Lily... I'm sorry it's come at such a lousy time, but I'm going to come and see you to make up for you not being able to come up here with Ma. They're going to give me a few days off.
Lily:	Thank you, sweetheart, I'm glad you can get back. Your Ma's bearing up and Annie's being a little darling, but it will be good to have you here. Your Pa's not saying nothing to no one.
Rose:	It somehow makes it more real to see his name on that form. It's so hard to keep working out here, knowing that Charlie's gone. Seeing all the soldiers' wounds I can't help but wonder what happened to him. You've got to try to forget until you get some time to yourself – I keep telling meself that every soldier I treat can go home to his family. Except when they're well they just send them back to fight again. Sometimes it all seems very stupid.

26th October

Walter:	Back home in Battersea. It does feel strange to be here – it's been nearly 3 months since we left for St Albans... nice to see everyone, even if it is a bit trying talking about Charlie. We ain't heard nothing about where he's been buried, if he has been. Don't like to think about it.

Mary: It's good to have you home, son. If I had my way I'd keep you here now.

Lily: We're all glad to have you back – and you look so different.

Walter: Do I? That's all the marching we been doing – we're all as fit as fleas.

Fred: You want to come up here and see the rest of us, Lil! Anyway, regards to your family, Walter – such rotten news. Sounds like our boys have been having a rough time at Ypres ever since.

29th October

Walter: I must say, as good as it is to see everyone, I'm actually looking forward to getting back to the boys at training. Yes, even you Fred…

Fred: Well we ain't missed you here so don't hurry! Just more marching… although we been doing a bit of practice with compasses too – even having to find places at night. I ain't too clever at it, if I'm honest. Here's a story that will make you laugh – I got meself lost the other night… I was supposed to be finding me way back to base with the compass (in the dark, mind) and was heading through this hedge thinking, 'this ain't right,' when all of a sudden there was a great snort and a stamping and I thought, 'blimey that's a bull!' So I set off the other way – well, I couldn't get out of the hedge at first, but then I ran for all I was worth. I didn't see him again, he must have been stuck behind that hedge, but I didn't let up running for about ten minutes. Got meself even more bleedin' lost. Sat on a fence and thought, 'this would never happen to Walt…' In the end I saw a light and heard someone calling out me name. Worse luck, it was Sergeant 'Bighead' Bridges. Wouldn't let me hear the end of it – took us all out to 'my' field the next day, after I'd told everyone about this bull, and it was only a load of bleedin' cows. I reckon I must have scared that bull off. When are you back?

Walter: Crikey that made me laugh. Nice to have something to smile about. I'm back tomorrow, mate – we'll go and find that 'bull'. Ha ha. See you soon.

November 1914

1st November

Walter: You alright, Ed? Heard you got given a white feather.

Ed: You didn't have to make it public, Walt... To be honest I didn't know what was happening until the girl was almost in me pocket. I thought maybe she'd come over all friendly but then she said, "A skiver! A young, strong lad in civvies!" and some other ladies came over and laughed at me too. Then the first one took out a white feather and stuck it in me lapel to say I was a coward. I started to say me big brother was only just killed but I choked a bit and they laughed even more.

Suddenly producing a large white feather, she jabbed it into his waistcoat. And in another tone, fierce and scornful, she added:..."You coward! Why don't you enlist?"

Walter: I'm sorry to hear it, brother. I don't know what to make of it – I always thought you should sign up but I don't know if I've changed me mind, what with Charlie gone. What a rotten thing. Did it make you want to enlist?

Ed: Of course it did – I went straight to the recruiting office, stood outside looking at it... then the sergeant came out and said, "Alright, sonny? Think you fancy wearing khaki now? About time too!" and I suddenly thought of Charlie and I scarpered. I still ain't going, Walt. They can give me enough feathers to make a fan if they like, I ain't going.

Margaret: Your poor mother, I don't know how she bears the shame. I know that if one of my boys were to give his life in the line of duty it would make his brother only more keen to take up the fight. It is a great pity, I think, that the country has come to this – young men skulking about on street corners, waiting to be called up. Keep that white feather as a lesson, Edward, and go and fight in your brother's name.

Ed: I weren't skulking! I was crossing the Chelsea Bridge. And anyway I chucked that feather over the side. With any luck it's halfway to Belgium itself by now.

2nd November

Walter: At least the Territorial Force is doing well in Belgium! The first lot of Terriers out there, the London Scottish, was sent on Halloween to fill a gap in the line. They had to fight hard to hold a ridge at Messines – pushed the Germans back twice but got broke through in the end. Bought some time anyway, even though they was outnumbered and their weapons and ammo weren't working right. Well done lads.

Ed: I don't know about well done – I heard they went out with 700 men and came back with 300.

3rd November

Walter: Heard there was a German naval attack on Great Yarmouth – always puts the wind up you a bit when they get that close. They only managed to shell the empty beach though, silly chaps. The town was fine and our British destroyers saw them off. They ought to know better than to mess with us! Seems they laid a few mines though.

John: I told you our Navy was the best in the world! This is a picture of the crew of HMS Lively (one of the ships that sent the enemy packing). I like the ship's dog.

4th November

Walter:	Well, we're leaving St Albans… but not to go to the Western Front, or even the Eastern Front… just Luton. More training. Have to say we're getting fed up. We're fit as we can be and at full war strength – about 950 men – but still no word of when we can get started. It don't look like the war will be over by Christmas neither, so you can bet they need us out there. And now to have to leave our nice billets here and move everything out to Luton. It ain't easy anyway as the whole lot's got to move with us – administration, stores, tents… it'd be just as easy to get to Le Havre!
Fred:	It'd be over by Christmas if they sent us out there, Walt. As long as they ain't relying on me and a compass.
Walter:	Too right – I'd finish off the lot of them in Charlie's name and make it back in time to hang the mistletoe.
Fred:	But we're going to Luton instead.
Walter:	That's right.

5th November

Walter:	It's Guy Fawkes Night and we're banned from having a bonfire! It ain't fair. I always loved going down to see it with everyone back home. Remember that time we climbed all over it before they lit it Fred? Thought we'd find some treasure someone had thrown out… ha ha.
Fred:	That's right! We was eight or something. Came away with a butter pat, two empty tea boxes and a rear end full of splinters.
Lily:	Don't worry, there's no bonfire back here neither. I suppose we don't want to call the Zeppelins over. Oh, but someone made a Guy that looked like the Kaiser and that made everyone laugh. I've heard a couple of fireworks go off too but it's only kids playing – everyone else is steering clear of anything to do with gunpowder and whizzbangs. Never mind… next year we'll have a great big one, eh?

6th November

Walter: Just heard I'm part of the Advance Party heading to Luton… our Company Sergeant Major caught me by surprise just as I was leaving the dining hall and told me. Can't say no of course. Means I got to help out with getting everything over there before the rest of you jammy lot (Fred!) come over in a few days. Disappointed I won't get to see all the St Albans people come out to wave us off with the band and all that, but we're going to have the cooks, blacksmiths and all sorts with us – maybe I can talk them into bringing the best food for the journey! We'll have a bit of transport, but other than that it'll be marching again – more than 20 miles. Good job we're all fit. The other day we marched nearly 24 miles in full marching order and with a blanket and ground sheet each.

Fred: Get us the best billets, won't you Walt!

Lily: Send me your new address when you get there sweetheart, I've a letter to send to you.

Walter: Thanks, Lil, I will do. It'll be nice to get a letter.

7th November

Walter: Said goodbye to Mr and Mrs Abbott, Miss Sarah and the boys today – I'm a bit sad about it if I'm honest. Still, can't grumble, as they gave me a fruit cake to take with me! Ha ha. Will have to see where we're billeted in Luton. Hope it's as nice as here – they've looked after me very well.

Jane: Just to say we shall miss you very much Walter – you and Bert have become quite a part of the family. I know Jimmy for one will be very lost without his 'big brother'! Do write to us, as you said you would, and I hope you find nice lodgings in Luton. With all our very best wishes for the future (and enjoy the cake!), The Abbotts.

Walter: Thanks, Mrs A. Tell Jimmy and Jack to be good and I'll write to you all soon.

10th November

Mary: How are you getting on in Luton, Walter? We're getting by here, but it's hard when we can't have a funeral for your brother. I had a letter of condolence from his Company Commander, which was nice to get but don't make it easier. Your father's even quieter than normal. Well, I thought you might like a bit of news from London – it was the State Opening of Parliament today and some Indians who fought at Ypres was there! The crowd all cheered them. It seems they stepped in when our army was low on numbers and helped us to get ahead in the battle.

Walter: Thanks, Ma. Sorry I ain't had a moment to write – we been so busy trying to find billets for everyone here in Luton. I've not done too bad though – stopping with two nice old ladies. I think they must be sisters. Good to hear about the Indian fellows. Sounds like a lot of the Empire countries have been fighting hard.

Rose: We see so many Indian soldiers here in Boulogne. We had a trainload the other day who all had smashed left arms from a machine gun that caught them while they was firing over a trench. Lots was 47th Sikhs with their long hair under their turbans – never seen nothing like it. If there's one good thing about the war, it's getting to meet all sorts of people.

12th November

Walter: How are you getting on, Rose?

Rose: Hello, Walt. Not bad now, thanks – we've had a rest day and at last a full night's sleep. I'd been in the same clothes for 40 hours before that! I'm glad the fighting has eased up a bit, it's been very tough going. We've been up and down on the ambulance train from Boulogne, collecting the wounded from motor ambulances near the Front. We care for them here a while and sometimes we ship them back home for more treatment. There's been some very bad ones – it's horrible how smashed-up a man can get from shellfire. But they're such sweethearts, they don't whine or moan or nothing. One chap turned out to have a break in his thigh bone that he didn't even mention because it weren't so bad as his poor shoulder what he'd broke. He'd rigged it up with his rifle as a splint and padded it with bits of his mate's kilt!

Mary: Good to hear you're having a rest… I sent up a parcel with a newspaper and some things for the men. I hope it arrives soon.

Rose: It arrived today! Thank you for it – the men will go barmy over the chocolate and cigs. Newspapers we don't do too badly for – we even get the same day's Daily Mail from Folkestone! It don't always match up with the news we get back from the Front though. On the worst days at Ypres it just said the fighting was 'severe'. When you're lifting all them heavy men onto the top bunks in the ambulance train, each one bleeding faster than you can stop it and then you find they're dead before you can treat them… well, you start to think they need new words for this type of thing – 'severe' don't cover it. 'Hell', more like. I had a chap with both eyes gone from a shell wound. He lived, mind.

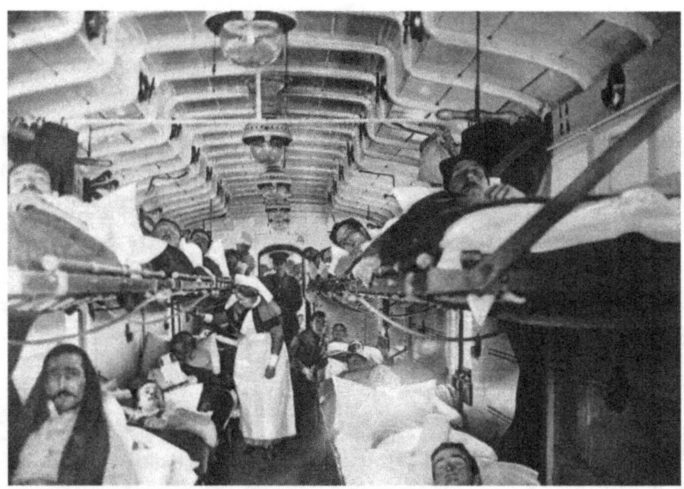

14th November

Lily:	I don't like to tell you Walt, but Herb's been back in Arding & Hobbs wanting to have a word with me. I get ever so worried in case I find him waiting for me outside after work, but I think he's more of a gentleman than that. The other girls rather like him – he's tall. Mrs Reed said they ought to put a sign in the window saying I'm not for sale.
Walter:	Gentleman my foot! I don't care if he's 8 foot tall, don't you talk to him no more. Didn't he see your badge?
Lily:	I showed him it! He didn't seem to think too much of it. Anyway, Mrs Reed chased him off in the end. I do miss you, Walt.
Walter:	Well I'm glad she did. I miss you too, sweetheart. Chin up though, eh? It won't be long.

15th November

Walter:	Happy Birthday Ed! Sorry you've had a rough time lately. What you up to today?
Ed:	Thanks, Walt. Had a present this morning – well, two really – Ma knitted me a new pair of socks. And little Annie wrote me a card all by herself. She read it out loud to me in the end before I could even get a look at it. She ain't half getting clever. I need them socks today and all as I've got a job down on Tregarvon Road. Fellow wants his sash windows fixed up before it gets too cold. He's got two sons away in the army and he's that nervous about it – don't blame him – I was going to say about our Charlie but I thought I wouldn't in the end.
Walter:	Poor fellow. Best you don't say nothing. Well, have a happy birthday then Ed, even if it is mending windows. At least you have warm feet!

16th November

Walter: Sounds like our soldiers fighting out in Africa have had some trouble with their horses – they ain't never seen a camel before and it spooks them! The picture in the Mirror made me laugh. To be honest, I ain't seen a camel neither, so I mightn't be any better. There's been a lot of fighting out there – must get confusing with the different colonies belonging to different European countries.

GETTING HORSES ACCUSTOMED TO CAMELS ON THE SANDY WASTES OF AFRICA.

GETTING HORSES ACCUSTOMED TO CAMELS ON THE SANDY WASTES OF AFRICA.

The camel's appearance is evidently against him as far as the horse is concerned, as the cavalrymen in Africa have to accustom their mounts to the presence of these unwieldy-looking beasts, which are very useful in the great sandy tracts. The horse in the picture reared and pranced as soon as the camel came in view and tried to run away.

17th November

Walter: Ma, I know it ain't me birthday for ages yet, but you know how you knitted them socks for Ed? Well, some of the lads' mothers have been sending some up here… do you think you could knit me some too? I get cold feet. Not on marches, but it's the standing around that does it. Don't worry yourself or nothing but just if you get a bit of time.

Rose: Oh Ma, to have some woollen socks! Do you think you could send some out here too? It gets so cold out here now with these frosty nights. The worst is on the ambulance trains – we managed to rig up a little stove heater in the corridor, but it don't do much and everyone's toes is cold as ever. After a long night we always look out for the sun coming up over the woods as we go by, thinking it'll warm things up, but it don't. Makes me miss that heatwave we had back in Battersea in July. Feels like a lifetime ago.

Mary: Alright alright, I'll knit you all some! I expect you nurses could do with some warm underthings as well, so I've said as much to the other ladies in the street and hopefully we'll have a nice lot to send out to you both. Mrs Wiggins weren't too keen, there's a surprise, but I'll see if I can talk her round.

Day Sock

MEASUREMENTS OF FINISHED SOCK.—Length from top of sock to bottom of heel, 14½ inches. Length of foot, 11 inches. Length of ribbing, 4½ inches. Length of leg to commencement of heel, 12 inches.

The 11-inch sock is the size mostly required, but it is recommended that the feet be made fully large to sizes to allow for shrinkage. Socks are issued to the Army in the following proportions:

9½-inch	11-inch	11½-inch	
Slender Men's 181	Men's 683	Outsize Men's 136	Per 1,000 pairs

MATERIALS REQUIRED.—Six ounces 3-ply Wheeling or 4-ply Fingering: four steel knitting needles, No. 12 for Wheeling, and No. 13 for Fingering.

Cast on 68 stitches; rib 4½ inches, 2 plain, 2 purl; knit plain 7½ inches (12 inches in all).

HEEL.—Knit plain 34 stitches on to one needle; *turn*, purl back these 34 stitches; *turn*, knit plain; repeat these two rows (always slipping the first stitch) sixteen times (17 in all).

With the inside of the heel towards you: purl 19 stitches, purl 2 together, purl 1.

Turn, knit 6 stitches, slip 1, knit 1, pull slipped stitch over, knit 1, *turn*, purl 7 stitches, purl 2 together, purl 1.

Turn, knit 8 stitches, slip 1, knit 1, pull slipped stitch over, knit 1, *turn*, purl 9 stitches, purl 2 together, purl 1.

Turn, knit 10 stitches, slip 1, knit 1, pull slipped stitch over, knit 1, *turn*, purl 11 stitches, purl 2 together, purl 1.

Turn, knit 12 stitches, slip 1, knit 1, pull slipped stitch over, knit 1, *turn*, purl 13 stitches, purl 2 together, purl 1.

Turn, knit 14 stitches, slip 1, knit 1, pull slipped stitch over, knit 1, *turn*, purl 15 stitches, purl 2 together, purl 1.

Turn, knit 16 stitches, slip 1, knit 1, pull slipped stitch over, knit 1, *turn*, purl 17 stitches, purl 2 together, purl 1.

Turn, knit 18 stitches, slip 1, knit 1, pull slipped stitch over, knit 1.

THE BRITISH RED CROSS SOCIETY

Pick up and knit 18 stitches down the side of the heel piece. Knit the 34 stitches of the *front* needles (on to one needle). Pick up and knit the 18 stitches at the other side of the heel piece. Divide the heel stitches on to the two side needles, and knit right round again to the centre heel.

First needle: knit to within 3 stitches of the front end of side needle, knit 2 together, knit 1.

Front needle plain.

Third needle: knit 1, slip 1, knit 1, pull slipped stitch over, knit plain to end of needle.

This reducing to be done every other row until there are 68 stitches on the needles (front needle 34, side needles 17 each).

Knit plain until the foot (from the back of the heel) measures 2½ inches *less* than the full length required, viz.: (a) 8½ inches for the 11-inch sock; (b) 9½ inches for the 11½-inch sock.

To DECREASE FOR THE TOE.—Begin at the *front* needle; knit 1, slip 1, knit 1, pull slipped stitch over, knit plain to within 3 stitches of the end of the needle, knit 2 together, knit 1.

Rose:	Thanks Ma! We'll be glad of them. I always think if it's so cold here, then what must it be like in the trenches? They don't have much more than what they came out with in August, so Heaven knows how they keeps warm. Knit as much as you can!
Walter:	Thanks, Ma. I'll look out for a parcel.
Lily:	Count me in – perhaps I could come round after work, Mrs Carter? I ain't too bad at knitting.
Mary:	You're welcome anytime, Lily.

18th November

Rose:	Some good news! We're getting electric lights and heating in our ambulance train! That will make a difference, although we'll still need those socks. We was at Le Havre yesterday – the ships coming to take the wounded back home couldn't get into Boulogne because of the rough weather, so we had to take the train further down and put them off at Le Havre. Had a look around to see what dear old Charlie would have seen when he arrived in France. Not much time for that though – there's always something doing. A nurse there told me we'd brought them a rum lot. I didn't have the heart to tell her we'd already put off the worst ones further up. The men are all being very brave and kind, thanking everybody very much because this rotten hospital is the nicest place they been for months…
Walter:	Crikey, electric lights eh? You'll be glad of that. No chance of it here with my two old ladies. I think everything in their house comes straight out of the 1860s– flowery William Morris stuff everywhere. What are the lads out there saying about the fighting?
Rose:	Oh, it's all they talk about. A fellow will come in with both legs blown off and all he talks about with the others is how they can stop Fritz getting to Calais. I reckon they've seen too much of the war and now all they care about is keeping it away from England. Don't blame them. I don't know

how they'll manage it though – we get reports one day saying the enemy has been pushed back, then the next day someone says they've got 80,000 reinforcements from somewhere and will be at Calais by the 10th of December. I couldn't tell you which way it's going to go.

Ed: Sounds pointless to me, all this to-ing and fro-ing… kill off 80,000 men, send in 80,000 more…

21st November

Walter: Great news in the Express – they say Lille has been retaken by the British. The fellow in the paper reckons we'll have seen off Fritz and be celebrating by Christmas! A shame not to get out there of course, but it would be good to get it all over with before the end of the year.

Fred: Imagine doing all this training for nothing! But you're right, good news.

Rose: I'd wait and see if I was you. We've not heard too much about it here, apart from that the Germans in Lille had an outbreak of typhoid fever – maybe that's why they left. Besides, I heard they're advancing into what used to be Poland, so it ain't over yet… If you find Lodz on a map, to the west of Warsaw, that's where they are.

22nd November

Mary: It's five weekends before Christmas and all us ladies in the road are preparing our Christmas puds. It don't feel right to be missing three children… Annie says she'll give an extra stir and make a wish for each of you, as you can't – and she says she'll eat some for you too! We've got all sorts in it – currants, almonds, nutmeg, carrots… and a little porter beer as we can't afford no brandy.

Rose: Oh Ma, you don't know what you're doing to my stomach! What I'd give for some Christmas pud… and thanks so much for the socks and woolly underthings. They arrived this morning and everyone's a bit happier all of a sudden!

Mary: You're very welcome! We did enjoy making them and I'm glad the post got to you so quick. Nice to know we can do something for you out there.

23rd November

John: Quick bit of news. The British have entered Basra (in Mesopotamia). They're going to keep the oil pipeline safe so the Navy will have enough fuel.

24th November

Walter: It do make a difference to have these new rifles – we been given converted Long Lee Enfields, so now they take the Mark VII cartridge with a pointed bullet. Can't say nothing good about the ammo though. Been doing field firing out at Dunstable and got some ammunition from America. It all comes in loose cardboard boxes and I'd say about 1 in 10 is a misfire…

Fred: At least! It don't half make things hard. I reckon I gets all the duds specially too.

26th November

Rose: Thought I'd let you know at home – the fighting seems to have gone fairly quiet out here. I don't know whether it's because of the cold or because the Russians are coming through from the east. Or maybe we've won? Ha. Who knows. I suppose they'd soon tell us. Very glad not to have to treat as many wounds and breaks, but now we're seeing all the other sicknesses that the poor men get from being in freezing cold trenches. Rheumatism, a lot of them, and then we had two fellows with frost bite. One of them looks likely to lose his whole foot. The worst though is an odd thing – a boy (he can't be more than 16) who's in a kind of shock. He don't know where he's at, poor lad – you ask him his name and all he can manage to do is look right at you and say "Mother" over and over. It just about breaks your heart. The other fellows are being quite kind to him, being that he's young, but one of them said another man in his battalion cried off with the same thing and everyone reckoned he was just a coward. I don't know… this poor lad ain't pretending, that's for sure.

28th November

Walter: The paper says there's German refugees now as well as the Belgians and the French and all the others… part of me thinks it's good that they're getting a taste of their own medicine but then the other part remembers they're just ordinary folk who've lost their homes. I don't know what to make of it.

Rose: I think refugees are refugees, wherever they're from. We've had some trouble here with spies pretending that they're refugees – all nationalities, it don't seem to matter. I suppose they get paid to do it. The locals have been kindly putting people up and then finding them on the roof in the middle of the night, signalling to the Germans with lights or getting visits from carrier pigeons! Makes you feel bad for all the genuine chaps who won't be able to get a bed now. At least it's got a bit sunnier so they won't be quite so cold even if they have to sleep outside.

Walter: It'll be colder at night though, won't it, if it's clear? I didn't realise there was spies over there… they've got a nerve. Do they send them to jail?

Rose: They'd be lucky! It's straight to the firing squad for them… that's what they do with traitors out here. I get worried in case the lads with that shock are called traitors or deserters – some of the men have said that about our little lad who keeps asking for his mother.

GERMAN REFUGEES IN FLIGHT.

The Kaiser's beloved Prussia is beginning to experience some of the horrors of invasion which have been inflicted on Belgium. An endless procession of German refugees, fleeing before the advancing Russians, is seen in the above picture passing through the streets of Singen.

GERMAN REFUGEES IN FLIGHT

The Kaiser's beloved Prussia is beginning to experience some of the horrors of invasion which have been inflicted on Belgium. An endless procession of German refugees, fleeing before the advancing Russians, is seen in the above picture passing through the streets of Singen.

December 1914

1st December

Rose: Very exciting today – we've been at Wimereux, not far from Boulogne, and one of the trains that passed us had King George V himself on it! Word got out that he was in the restaurant carriage so we craned our necks but couldn't see him. We did have a laugh though – they've got the bridges covered with special blue and red curtains so His Highness don't get grubby! He should see the state of me. Ha ha. They say he's over here to visit HQ and see how we're all getting on. Good on him – though he'll see it all a bit quieter than it usually is.

Mary: How exciting, Rose. Do make sure you're neat, won't you, in case he comes by.

THE KING AT THE FRONT.

VISIT TO HEADQUARTERS OF THE BRITISH EXPEDITIONARY FORCE.

CHANNEL CROSSED IN A WARSHIP.

The King has gone to the front. This important and interesting announcement was made by the Press Bureau last night as follows :—

The King travelled over to France last night to visit the General Headquarters of the Expeditionary Force. He was accompanied by Lord Stamfordham and Major Wigram.

His Majesty and the members of his suite left Buckingham Palace at about three o'clock on Sunday afternoon, and proceeded to the coast, where a warship was in waiting to convey them across the Channel

and he had dismounted and put himself at the head of his troops. Addressing to them a few inspiriting words, he led them to the attack with much gallantry."

The net result was that the French troops were defeated and left 6,000 dead on the field.

Wars with France were fairly frequent in the early days of our history. Although both Henry VIII. and William III. touched French soil in their campaigns abroad, the last British monarch to see much actual service in France was Henry V. He organised two invasions, and famous battles, such as Agincourt, distinguished his campaigns. His attacks were finally ended by the Treaty of Troyes, under which he was recognised as heir and regent of France,

3rd December

Walter: Just seen this in the paper – there's so many foreign refugees over here now that the Express is going to translate its property adverts into French! Tres bien and all that.

Owing to the large number of French and Belgians now in this country, Furnished Room and Apartment Advertisements will be translated into French free of charge.

5th December

Lily:	Thought I'd show you, sweetheart – they're selling special wartime Christmas cards in the stationers! I know you ain't out at the Front or nowhere yet (although you might as well be, the amount I don't see you) but I thought I'd send you one anyway, being that you're my soldier. Any news on when you might go, or where?
Walter:	Hello Lil! And thanks, yes I should like to see one. I expect they've got them in Luton too but I've not seen them yet. Fred said he saw lots of flags strung up instead of tinsel though. It will be a strange Christmas if this don't blow over. I have to say I don't think it will now. No news on when or where we'll be going… might be France, might be Mesopotamia, might even be here in Britain. Wherever it is, I hope they get a move on, we've had some men leaving the battalion to take commissions because they're so fed up with waiting.
Lily:	Poor you, I'm not surprised you're fed up. Although I'm glad you ain't out in France… especially in this cold. Here's one of the cards anyway–

THOUGH WINTER'S COLD FREEZE ME

AND MAKE ME FEEL BLUE

THERE'S A WARM CORNER ALWAYS

IN MY HEART FOR YOU.

Walter:	Thanks, Lil. It's nice that.

7th December

Walter: How is it over there, Rosie? Did you see the king in the end?

Rose: No such luck Walt! Though I've had plenty of other things to keep me busy… I shall be quite the clever stick by the time I get out of here. You should hear the bits of Hindustani I've picked up – I got one of the lads here to teach me some words what I might need. Only problem is when they answer with something I don't know! They say 'chai' for tea (but most of us just call it 'char' and they understand that alright) and if something's nice it's 'khush' and if it's broke it's gone 'phut'. The best thing is seeing them all out on the quay cooking chupatties when we're stopped in Boulogne – it do smell nice. Did you hear two of them got the Victoria Cross for bravery too when King George was over?

Walter: Yes I heard about them – good lads.

9th December

Walter: Just heard about the sinking of the German cruisers off the Falkland Islands. They was trying to raid the port at Stanley but didn't bet on a big British squadron being there too… they tried to scarper of course but our ships can do 25.5 knots and theirs can only do 22.5 knots, so it weren't no contest really. The Nurnberg and the Dresden escaped but the Brits have set off after them too. This is our HMS Invincible picking up survivors from the SMS Gneisenau – they'll be prisoners now.

John: Our ships have bigger guns too – 12 inch against 8 inch. Don't I always tell you, you ought to have joined the Naval Reserve with me?

10th December

Walter: Heard there was some German submarines at Dover. Don't sound good. Any news, John?

John: No one's sure really, but it sounds like they tried to sneak into the harbour in the dark this morning. Probably trying to hit the warships there. The big guns at Dover saw them off though. Don't know how far off they went.

> Some warships were lying in the harbour at the time, and these were undoubtedly the object of the submarines' attack. The morning was very dark, and a rain haze favoured the attempts of the submarines to slip past the defenders.
>
> The effects of the gunnery were watched with keen interest by a number of people, who had hurried to the sea front at the first sound of the guns. The flashes of fire which stabbed through the darkness as the guns were rapidly swung round into various positions following the movements of the submarines had a weird effect.
>
> Powerful searchlights swept the surface of the sea from the piers and breakwaters. As soon as the firing started the vessels of the destroyer flotilla were busily on the move, and soon steamed to sea to take part in the repelling of the submarines.

Mary: I don't like how close they're getting.

Walter: Don't worry, they couldn't even reach the town at Great Yarmouth and now the guns have scared them off at Dover. They can mess about in the sea as much as they want, they won't get near us.

11th December

Lily: Just finished me shift at Arding & Hobbs, came out and found the crossroads all jammed up! All the tramcars have stopped and their lights gone out. No one knows how to get home and it's pouring with rain. Is it the same anywhere else?

Ed: Hi Lil, I'm on a job up Camden way and it's the same here. Trams not moving and people just sitting on them in the dark wondering what to do. Don't know how I'll get back to Battersea, especially with me tool bag. The driver says there's nothing coming through the overhead wires, so I reckon something must have happened at the generating station. Soaking rain here as well. Just when I thought I was on me way home for dinner…

Walter: Bad luck, Ed – bet you wish you had a motor. Are you alright lily? Hope you didn't get too cold.

Lily: Oh I'm alright, I'd only be walking anyway. It's the folks who've got to get back out to the suburbs that'll have trouble – there's no trains out to some of them places. They was all trying to pack themselves into the omnibuses but they couldn't fit.

Walter: How are you getting on now, Ed? Do you think you'll get home?

Ed: Well I overhead the driver and conductor saying they don't think it'll be fixed before the morning and they're going to sleep in the tram. Reckon I'll join them, if they'll let me. There's a few lady typists on board, so it ain't all bad…

Mary: I've always said you can't trust electricity! I suppose I shall have to save you your dinner, Ed. I'll put it in the meat safe – it's cold enough outside – and you can have it when you get back. No sense wasting food.

Mabel: They're rigging up some of the trams with lanterns here so nothing crashes into them. Good idea. My Ma says all of London's the same except for Forest Hill and Lewisham – they get their electricity from Deptford, not Greenwich, so they're alright.

14th December

Rose: Finally seeing soldiers with proper clothes for keeping the cold out. They been given these lovely fur coats made out of all sorts – sheep skin, goat skin – and they can't stop talking about how warm they are. They're walking around looking like great bears! Except some of them ain't quite sure how to wear them and keeps the fur on the inside. No such luck for the feet – a Scotch chap told me the rain and the mud is so bad that some of them have given up on their brogues and socks and are wading through the mud in their bare feet! I told him I'd never heard nothing so daft and he said, "Ah, but lassie, skin is light, portable and easy to clean." Couldn't argue with him...

December 1914

16th December 1914

Walter: How's this for an early Christmas present? I've been put up for promotion! Lance Corporal Carter, Second-in-Command of a Rifle Section! How does that sound? Ha ha. I'm made up. They said it's for 'reliability', 'turnout' and 'weapon handling'. I get a stripe and all.

Lily: Oh sweetheart I'm so proud of you! What a thing. I'm going to tell all the girls at the shop – and Herbert – Lily Howes is courting a Lance Corporal! Well done, darling.

Mary: Such wonderful news! Your Pa's perked up for the first time since we heard about Charlie. He's everso proud of you Walt. Oh I can't wait to tell Mrs Wiggins next door – that'll teach her to be so high and mighty. What does it mean though? Will your duties change?

Walter: Well, we'll be doing the same things as normal but I'll be supervising a few men now. Each Section has 12 men in it, see, including me and the Section Corporal – he's the one above me – though it'll probably still be me that gets in trouble if we ain't doing well! I do get to supervise work parties instead of being in them though, so there's something… and if anything ever happened to the Corporal, I'd have to take over.

Mary: Well I'm blowed, that really is something. Well done, love!

Walter: Thanks Ma. I'm a bit nervous about it if I'm honest… just don't tell the lads! I'll let you know how I get on.

17th December

Walter: Fuming! The enemy has shelled some towns on the coast – yesterday they bombed Scarborough, Whitby and the Hartlepools and there's hundreds dead and wounded. That just ain't right, attacking innocent civilians who ain't got nothing to do with it. Don't know what our Navy was playing at neither, letting them get away with it. The paper says our lot chased after them but was too late. I'll say. We need more dreadnought battleships – they'd have finished them off.

Mary: It's rotten, Walt. When I think of all them children and mothers killed and people's homes destroyed it breaks my heart. And just before Christmas too. I ain't half glad we're not near the coast, although what if they come sailing up the Thames?

Walter: They won't do that, Ma – they'd be sitting ducks. I'll tell you something though, what with Charlie and then this I ain't got no sympathy for Fritz no more. Get Lance Corporal Carter out there – he'll show them what's what.

Fred: Oho, do excuse me Mr Second in Command of a Rifle Section! You're right though, we won't let them get away with this.

19th December

Rose: Hold on to your hats, I've learnt some more language. It's French – 'chauffage' – means heating. And I only know it because ours is broke. So now I've got to work through the night in the freezing cold in this rotten hospital train. And when I'm not working I'm trying to sleep while the train rattles along and nearly shakes me out of me bunk. And you daren't grumble because it still ain't near as bad as the trenches… I don't know how they stick it out there. Rum and cigs I suppose.

Ma: I told you it weren't going to be fun and games.

Rose: I didn't want it to be fun and games! I just think they ought to sort out the 'chauffage'. For the men more than us. We've been using hot bricks for warmth but it ain't no good. And we had a whole new set of wounded in. Looks like the fighting's getting going again, and in all this mud! Rain and rain and more rain…

20th December

Walter: Any better today sis?

Rose: Thanks for asking, but no not much… although I see why I was out of sorts yesterday – I've hatched a rotten cold. Not surprising really. No time off, especially now that we're down to three nurses per train instead of four. I managed to swap me night shift so I can get some sleep, but I have to make up for it in the day. We're rushed off our feet. And it seems every fellow coming through is going septic – that's where the wound gets infected and goes bad. It's so horrible – if there's a couple of days on the train before we can get them off to the hospital you can just watch it spreading up their leg or arm or wherever. Even the emergency amputations and trephinings (look it up if you ain't squeamish) coming in from the Casualty Clearing Stations is septic. No wonder, with the conditions out there. I can tell by a sort of instinct now before I even examine them what their chances are as you can tell a septic from the swelling under the bandages (and the smell – I never want to smell that again as long as I live) and you can tell a gangrene because he'll be greyish in the face. We treats that with incisions and injections of H_2O_2. Or amputation, if it's a limb. Here's hoping we get a break over Christmas.

Walter: That don't sound too good, Rosie. Sorry you're feeling rotten – hope it eases up a bit soon.

Rose: Thanks, Walt. Hope you're alright over in Luton and good luck with your new duties. Back to work now…

21st December

Walter: Winston Churchill, the First Lord of the Admiralty, has called the enemy 'baby-killers', after all them children was killed in Scarborough and Whitby and the Hartlepools. Sounds like a name that'll stick...

Ed: They keep saying about this 'baby-killing' – German soldiers bayoneting children and that – but I reckon it ain't true. I reckon they just tells us that to make you lot want to fight them.

Lily: I can't help but think that too, Ed. But they did shell all them families on the coast...

22nd December

Walter: Well, my two old ladies in Luton are set on having a Christmas tree so it's my job to go out and drag one back from the market... I had to lift out all their dusty old decorations too – looks like they've kept them since Christmas trees first came over, 70-odd years ago. It's a German thing though, ain't it, Christmas trees? Don't know how I feel about that.

Lily: They must be flash, to have a tree! We're making paper chains stuck together with flour and water... and my Ma got hold of some tinsel. We've put it round the fireplace – you should see it. We'll put some socks up there too, for Christmas Eve, though I'll have to darn a few so the nuts don't fall out. I wouldn't worry about German trees my love... decorate it with Union Jacks or something.

Walter: That's a grand idea! There's a lot of them in the shops. You're a clever one, Lil.

23rd December

Lily: We're off to Electric Avenue in Brixton to see the Christmas lights! I wish you could come, Walt... I can't get over all them electric lights in one place. There ain't so many this year of course, but Mabel says they've made a good effort. I asked your Ma if I could take Annie but she said it'd be too much for her with all the people. Such a shame for her, dear little one. I'll see if I can pick her up a little present while I'm there.

Walter: Thanks, Lil. Be careful though, won't you? Stick with your family. Brixton's full of them actor-types from the West End nowadays.

24th December

Rose: We're made up here – everyone's had a Christmas card from the King and Queen and the men have had presents from Princess Mary! She sent them each a tin with treats in. There's two choices – one for smokers and one for non-smokers and the younger boys. The tin for smokers has a pipe, tobacco, cigs, a tinder lighter and a picture of the Princess in it, and the other one has sweets, a writing case, a lead pencil made to look like a bullet and the same picture. The men are over the moon – they weren't expecting anything so it's been a nice surprise. She sent some sweets and spices for the Indian troops too. Bless her heart – they say she wanted to pay for it all out of her own allowance but it was too much, so she set up a fund and collected all the money to do it.

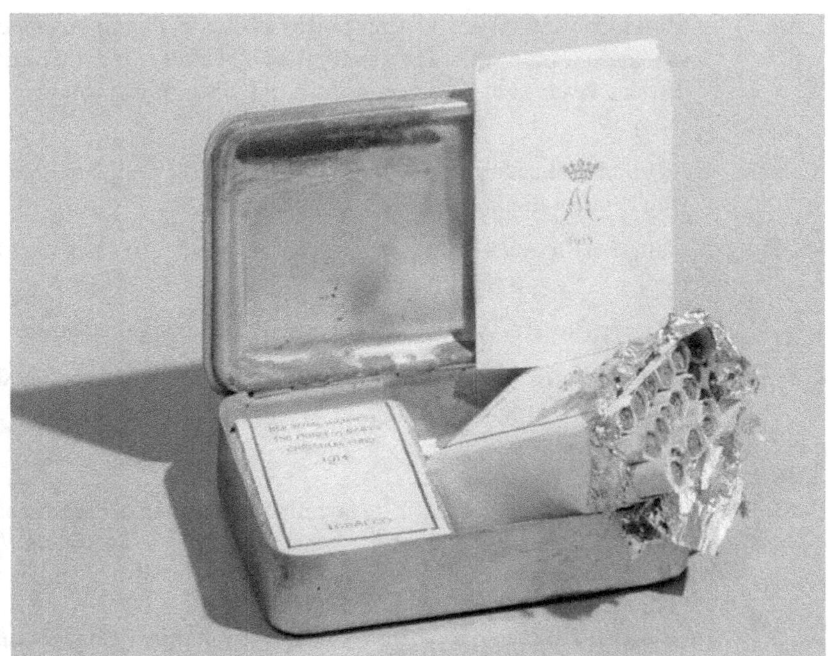

25th December

Walter: Merry Christmas everyone! Feels strange though, don't it? There's candles lit and some carol singers out but it's not the same. There's too many people missing. Last year we was all back home together – Charlie and Ed, Rose, me, Annie, Ma and Pa. Charlie was always jammy and got the silver thrupenny bit in the pudding. It don't half feel like a long time ago. Have you got a chicken this year, Ma? One of my old ladies here, Agnes, is making a right clatter in the kitchen but I bet her stuffing don't live up to yours. We get a meal with the Terriers as well though, so I'll be stuffed to the gills by this evening! I wonder if they'll get some good grub at the Front today. Hope they get some rest at least… I don't know if I could fight a man on Christmas Day. Oh, and thanks for the writing paper – it arrived this morning. I promise I'll use it.

Ma: A Merry Christmas to you too, love! We're back from church now – it was a long sermon what with talking about the past year, but the carols brightened us all up. And now it's very quiet here at Sabine Road. We do have a chicken, but just a little one this year. Annie's excited though, bless her heart. Her poor little legs mean she can't rush about like the other children, but she was sat on your old bed this morning with Ed and he was helping her to go through her stocking, fetching out the orange and the raisins. It was a good sight. Ed's becoming such a good boy since the shock with Charlie… but he still says he won't go to war. Well, it ain't the time for that kind of talk. Have a good day, Walt, we do miss you.

Rose: Merry Christmas! And thanks for the post, Ma. Shampoo powder is all a girl could want out here and everyone will be pinching it. The orderlies are drunk already though, so goodness knows how much work we'll get done today...

Mabel: All good wishes to you and your family, Walt! Say hello to Fred for me too won't you – tell him 'Happy Christmas'.

Fred: Well, there's a turn up... Happy Christmas yourself! That's made my day that.

Lily: A Merry Christmas all! Especially you, darling Walter. Missing you here...

Walter: I miss you all too. Have a happy day, won't you? I'll see you for Christmas dinner later, Fred...

26th December 1914

Walter: Of all the rotten cheek...! Late last night we had an order to mobilise. Had to head off with full equipment, all the way back to St Albans. We wasn't exactly fit for marching, having just had our Christmas dinner at the Plait Hall on Waller Street and not being what you'd call sober... but we set off and didn't do too bad. We marched ten miles, then got on a train that didn't move nowhere. People was saying things like the Germans was going to shell Essex and we was going to defend it – THEN Captain Wright turns up with old Bighead Bridges, who could barely stand straight for laughing, and tells us they was only pulling our leg and to get back out and march back to Luton! It was all a big joke! Not a funny one neither.

Fred: I reckon they was trying to get us to walk off that dinner. And to think they went all the way there by motor! Bleedin, cheek of it. They'd better give us the rest of the day off...

Lily: Don't be cross, but I did laugh when I read that! You poor lads.

27th December

Rose: We've heard the most wonderful story here today, you won't believe it – a fellow who came in from the trenches said there was a sort of truce on Christmas Day! And what's more, the Germans started it! We thought he'd gone daft but he was very fixed on it and told us the whole story – more and more people was gathering around his bed to hear it as he went on...

He said he was on sentry duty on Christmas night and suddenly he heard a German fellow call out in perfect English, "Good morning and a Merry Christmas!" He said he nearly fell over with the shock of it. But they're only 40 yards away, and can always hear each other talking anyway, so why not? Anyway, his mates were sitting round a fire in the trench trying to keep warm, but they started peeking over the parapet to see what was going on. He said you could've blown them down with a feather when they saw the Germans putting Christmas trees and lights up along their trenches! He said some of our lot was saying they should shoot the lights out but no one did and Fritz got braver, keeping his head above the top of the trench and our boys did the same, hoping they wasn't going to get shot. Then one of the Germans started singing! And our soldier said they ended up singing songs all night, Germans and British both – one fellow playing along with a mouth organ on our side and a chap with a cornet on theirs. It was a beautiful night too, all starlit and frosty, he nearly choked up remembering it.

Then, at dawn, Fritz called over, "Happy Christmas, Tommy! No work today! No shooting!" and our lot didn't know what to make of it. But, and this is the best bit, a couple of brave chaps decided to take them at their word and got out of the trench. You wouldn't believe it, but that's what this fellow said. And then they all met up, in the middle of No Man's Land, like friends, and swapped tins of bully beef and jam for cigars and chocolate. Someone told him there was even a football match further up the line!

They had to be careful though – it was Saxon Germans that they had the truce with and this soldier said the Prussian Guard in the next set of trenches weren't too happy about it. But the most incredible thing is he showed us this scrap of paper where he'd had one of the German fellows write down his name and address so they could try to meet up after the war! Can you believe that? And his new friend told him how fed up they all are with the fighting, but that they know London has been captured and Russia has surrendered and the war will be over in three weeks. Poor fellow – our chap had to put him straight by showing him a Daily Mail… it seems they get told all sorts of lies over there.

Well, in the end the peace only lasted that one day… then they all gave each other fair warning and started firing again, and that's when our fellow got his wound. He says he can't help wondering if it was his new mate who fired the shot, and who knows, maybe he aimed for his hand specially? Anyway, I've been helping him write a letter about it to his Ma (because his right hand's gone) and I just had to show you this bit: 'I thought at the time if only Kaiser Bill and other big chiefs could only agree the same as Tommy Atkins and the German soldiers we could soon have peace all the world over. Just one more little incident.' Makes you think, don't it?

Walter:	What a story, Rose! You don't reckon he was pulling your leg?
Ed:	I reckon that's true. Human spirit, ain't it? Good on them.
Mary:	Well, it's a nice thought, love, but your father's calling it a disgrace – it's put him in a right temper thinking about anyone giving anything to a fellow who might've had something to do with Charlie.

29th December

Walter:	Thought I'd share this from the paper – tells you what to do if the Zeppelins make it to London… Make sure you read it Lily, and you Ma.

IF THE ZEPPELINS COME TO LONDON.

CIVILIANS WARNED TO TAKE COVER.

Should German aircraft ever reach London falling pieces of shell from the guns fired at the enemy might be as much a source of danger as the aviators' bombs.

A warning on this point was issued yesterday from Scotland-yard as follows:—

The naval and military authorities call the attention of persons using the streets to the danger from fragments of shell and from bullets from the guns used against hostile aircraft attempting a raid on London.

The civil population are warned to keep under cover, preferably in basements, upon hearing the sound of firing by guns or of explosives.

31st December

Lily:	This time last year you'd never have believed it, would you, if someone had told you everything that was about to happen? Here's hoping 1915 brings the end of this rotten war… of all wars, in fact. No nice New Year celebrations for any Germans or Austrians living on the British coast – even anyone with parents from them countries – as they're all getting kicked out of their homes and moved to special areas 30 miles inland. They've only been given a week to move! I reckon it's because of the shellings on the east coast – everyone's starting to think anyone who's even a little bit German is a spy.

ALIENS TO BE MOVED.

DRASTIC NEW ORDER FOR EAST COAST TOWNS.

NOTICE TO QUIT.

WOMEN AND BRITISH BORN DESCENDANTS INCLUDED.

The military and police authorities have at last taken drastic action against naturalised Germans and Austrians on the east coast, with a view to minimising the spy danger.

Notices to quit were served yesterday by the police, acting for the military authorities, on persons who are regarded as undesirable residents of coast towns in the Tyneside district. Those affected by the new regulations include:—

Alien enemies.

Naturalised aliens of both sexes.

British-born descendants of aliens, including the second generation.

January 1915

1st January

Walter: Happy New Year chaps, It's all go already for us... the 1/23rd are being changed into four companies (it's been eight until now). It's not going to change things too much – we been training together anyway because some companies are a bit short on numbers, and the Commanders and Seconds-in-Command will stay the same. Fred and I get to stay in the same company too, so that's alright.

Fred: Good job and all – wouldn't like to have different free time from you... I'd have to find someone else to tell rotten jokes to.

Walter: Here's one for you, Fred – not too far off me own rifle section...

2nd January

Walter: Rotten news about the sinking of HMS Formidable, and on New Year's Day too. They reckon they only saved 199 men out of 750. These German submarines are starting to put the wind up me...

4th January

Rose: We had a sergeant on the train today – going down to Le Havre. He said his battalion came out with 1,400 men and now there's only 78 left. Can you believe that? He was moaning about the new young officers who get too excited and won't keep their heads down when they're in the trench – they ain't got the experience because they been rushed in to fill the gaps. Another fellow told me the Germans have got officers now who've only been out 2 weeks… so I suppose it's the same all over.

7th January

Lily: Love, did you hear about 'Lassie' the dog? Bit of nice news for once. There was a sailor off the 'Formidable' who got pulled in from the sea at Lyme Regis and put in a mortuary because everyone thought he was a croaker… but the local pub had this crossbred collie dog called Lassie and she wouldn't leave him alone – kept licking his face and cuddling up to him – and he came around! Ain't that nice? You want to see if you can find yourself a little dog if you ever get out to the Front.

A.B. John Cowan, a Formidable survivor, with Lassie, who saved his life at Lyme Regis. The dog licked his face assiduously, thus inducing circulation.—(Daily Mirror photograph.)

DOG SAVES SAILOR'S LIFE.

AB John Cowan, a Formidable survivor, with Lassie, who saved his life at Lyme Regis. The dog licked his face assiduously, thus inducing circulation. - (Daily Mirror photograph)

Mabel: Oh Lil, that's so sweet! Makes you feel better don't it?

Rose: Look at her sleepy little face… I wouldn't mind getting a dog.

8th January

Walter: Looks like your fellow was right about the Christmas truce, Rose! Saw a story about it today. Ain't it funny that it's only just come out in the news? And only in the Mirror at that. Fred saw a local paper with a letter from the Front about it, but that's all. They say High Command was that angry about it they stopped all leave for the units that took part.

Ed: I suppose no one wants to say too much about it, in case everyone starts to think the Germans are actually friendly types who ain't worth killing… Funny that, ain't it? What if they all just stopped, and wouldn't fight each other no more?

Walter: Well, then Charlie would have died for nothing and I can't stand for that.

Ed: But if no one was fighting, he wouldn't have been killed in the first place…

Walter: He was in the Army, Ed, that was his job. And he was fighting for us and Ma and everyone at home. Don't talk no more about it, you're making me angry.

AN HISTORIC GROUP: BRITISH AND GERMAN SOLDIERS PHOTOGRAPHED TOGETHER.

Foes became friends on Christmas Day, when British and Germans arranged an unofficial truce. The men left the trenches to exchange cigars and cigarettes, and were even photographed together. This is the historic picture, and shows the soldiers of the opposing Armies standing side by side.

9th January

Walter: Have a look at this, Ed – from the Express today. Looks like you might not get a choice after all.

EVERY MAN MAY BE MADE A SOLDIER.

THE GOVERNMENT READY TO ADOPT COMPULSION IF NECESSARY.

"WE BAR NOTHING."

12th January

Rose: I'm that fed up with this rain. I suppose it can't be much better at home... but out here it somehow seems even more rotten. Just when you think there can't be no more rain left in the sky, it comes down all over again. Everywhere's flooded. We had a whole set of patients in the other day who were covered in mud exactly up to their necks! That's what they'd been wading through, poor loves. There's more than a few men drowned in it, and they can't get them out again when that happens... so they just stays the bottom of the trench. Best not to think about it.

Walter: Sounds like you're having a rough time Sis. I hope it dries up. Are the men still getting frost bite?

Rose: Not so much now, but their feet still have a hard time with the wet and the mud. They get all swollen and white. Lucky for them they usually can't feel them by that point – we work out how bad it is by pretending to talk to them and secretly sticking a needle in the bottom of their foot. If they don't yelp, then we know they ain't better yet.

Walter: I wish you hadn't told me that. I don't know how you keep it up, Rose. I hate feet. Ain't you squeamish?

Rose: I can't be squeamish, can I? You just get used to it. After everything I've seen, feet are nothing. You'll get used to it too, dearest Second-in Command of a Rifle Section, if you come out here.

Walter: I bleedin, well hope not. I hope they send me to Egypt with the Australians.

Rose: Well, then you'd get sunstroke instead. Remember that time you got burnt on the beach at Brighton and your nose looked like a beacon for a week? It'd be worse than that.

Walter: Thanks, Rose.

14th January

Walter: If you can, get hold of a copy of today's Express – 'Territorials Make a Fine Impression in India'. Good to hear the boys out there are doing us proud! To anyone who thought us Terriers weren't up to scratch, take a look at this – 'the Territorials turned out and marched with a swing and a precision hardly surpassed by highly-trained Regulars.' Seems the Indian winter is easier for them – sounds about right. It does make you fed up hearing about everyone else though and not being able to go out there yourself.

Fred: We'd do just as well if we was out there. Don't know why they still ain't getting us on ships…

Mary: Good to hear about the Terriers, Walter! I'm sure they'll have you out there in no time, not that it'll do my old nerves any good.

Lily: Great news, darling – well done them!

15th January

Mary: Saw this today – good idea to send some out there, keep their strength up.

Mabel: I've never been fond of meat lozenges… seems they can make anything into a lozenge these days. I like them peppermint and ginger ones mind, or a linseed one if I've got a cough.

17th January

Rose: I had a fellow on the ambulance train today who said one time in the trenches he went eleven weeks in the same clothes and without having a wash! Said he had to scrape himself off with a knife in the end… That'll teach me to moan when I don't have the time to get undressed for days. We've been so glad of that shampoo powder though, Ma, it makes you feel a bit more human… and smell a bit less human…

Mabel: Eleven weeks! That's rotten. He should've just stood out in all that rain.

Lily: And there's me whimpering about a cold wash over the basin every morning! Thank goodness for flannels.

19th January

Mary: Well, Mrs Wiggins is making sure everyone knows it's her birthday. She just swanned off down the street in a new hat and I'd swear I can smell roast beef cooking. I don't know where she gets it all from. Her husband's 'business', I'll bet. And here's me trying to get together some scrapings for your father's birthday tomorrow. It makes me cross. I did manage to get him a bit of relish for his scrambled eggs from down the road but it ain't much when you think about how hard he works, poor man. Still, we do what we can.

Walter: He'll be glad of it, Ma, don't worry. Wish him a happy birthday from me tomorrow.

Mary: I will do, Walt. Thank you.

20th January

Walter: More bad news – and on Pa's birthday too – the blasted Zeppelins have made it over here after all. Dropped bombs on Yarmouth and Kings Lynn last night… killed two people and smashed up a lot of houses. We ain't never had bombs from the sky before. And to think I was all excited about it last year. The paper's right though – the more damage they do, the more Brits want to join up. Serves them right.

23rd January

Walter: Have you heard about what they've done in Brighton? They've turned the big Royal Pavillion (you remember when we saw it, Lil? That day we went down on the train?) into a military hospital for the Indian soldiers who've been fighting for us. They've put in separate kitchens so they can make the right food for the Mohammedans and the Hindoos and the Sikhs, and they can pray in different places in the grounds too. They say the locals are going barmy over all things Indian all of a sudden – they've been collecting tunic buttons from any soldier who can spare one!

Lily: Yes, I remember – what a grand place! I'd like to see it now. I heard the mayor gave it over specially because he thought the décor would make the Indians feel at home… now there's more than 700 beds in it!

25th January

Walter: Well, they tried to bomb the coast again but our fellows in the Navy got their act together and didn't let them! Ha. We would have had another Scarborough on our hands but our lot broke the German code and worked out what they was up to. Hipper, their Admiral, thought he could sneak up on us with his measly 3 battle cruisers but Admiral Beatty came out of nowhere with 5 of ours and 6 light cruisers and extra destroyers! Old Hipper weren't expecting that! And our ships are faster too. They sunk the German ship Bluecher straight off. The rest got away but they won't have the nerve to try it again, I'll bet.

28th January

Walter:	The papers say they marched the survivors from the Bluecher through the streets of Edinburgh – I'll bet they got an earful!
Mary:	I hope they did! Rotten lot.
Walter:	The Mirror said they was wearing all sorts – not proper uniform and that. If that's all we're fighting against, I don't know how we ain't won yet.
Ed:	That's it, Walt… didn't you know? Whoever has the best uniform wins the war…
Walter:	Well it helps, don't it? If you ain't got the right kit you're going to get cold and wet and miserable. And you can't say we don't look smart.
Rose:	Oh, I suppose all the soldiers I see out here were smart as anything when they first came out, but you just can't keep it that way when you're living in a trench or in a boat or whatnot.

February 1915

1st February

Walter:	Strange news from the Eastern Front yesterday – they say the Germans used a type of poison to fight off the Russians, but they put it in a gas. Didn't work – the gas got froze up because it was too cold. Weird though, ain't it? Don't like to think about it…
Fred:	That gives me the creeps, that does. Would you breathe it in then?
Walter:	I suppose so. I've had good practice standing next to you on manoeuvres though – I can hold me breath at the first sniff of deadly gas!
Fred:	I might have saved your life there, mate.

4th February

Walter:	Poor old Turks, eh? Tried to get across the Suez Canal in Egypt to attack our lot and didn't get too far. They wasn't expecting the firepower. All sorts we had – Indians, Gurkhas, even Australians and New Zealanders, all on our side. The enemy ran back into the desert – don't know how they'll get on there, there ain't no water.
Rose:	We get Gurkhas on our hospital trains sometimes. I like them – they're everso brave and don't moan at all, but they do have a bad habit of taking off their underthings if they have lice (which is always, we all have lice out here) and throwing them out of the train window! We're running out of spares to give them…
Mary:	Rose! For the last time, we don't want to hear about underpants. Or lice. I hope you're getting on alright. Why don't you tell us how the weather is?
Rose:	Well it's cold, which at least makes the lice a bit calmer… sorry Ma. It has got a bit more like Spring over the last couple of days – sunshine and that. You'd like to see the honeysuckle east of Rouen, it's got leaves on already.

5th February

Walter: This don't sound good, Ma... Germany's going to 'blockade' us with them submarines. They say all the sea around us is going to be a war zone, starting 2 weeks from yesterday. I suppose they're trying to starve us. And they ain't going to hold back on neutral ships neither – they say they might get caught in 'accidents'.

Ed: Serves us right, really – we're the ones being crafty by putting neutral flags on war ships.

Walter: Are we? Didn't hear nothing about that. It's no good for Germany to fire on ships like that though – not when there might be civilians in them.

Ed: There might be, there might not be... that way we can use the civilians to protect the ships. Don't seem right to me.

GERMANY'S WAR ON NEUTRAL SHIPS.

WORLD INDIGNATION AGAINST THE THREATENED SUBMARINE OUTRAGES.

AMERICAN PROTEST PROBABLE.

FANTASTIC RUBBISH TALKED AND WRITTEN IN GERMANY ABOUT THE DOOM OF BRITAIN.

8th February

Rose: Well today's been a turn up for the books! Ha ha. I'm almost a bit shy to say it... I met a very charming Scotchman on our train today, and the best thing is, he asked for my address so he can write to me when we're all done with this fighting! But now I don't know what to do... we're not allowed to talk with patients like that. I told him I'd think about it, and I'm back in the nurses' quarters now, but he's only on the train until tomorrow (we're putting him off at Boulogne) so I have to make a decision. I might make one of the others do his dressings in the morning – I don't ever feel shy about them things but with him I think I would!

Lily: Oh Rosie that's exciting! What's his name? Does he wear a kilt? Oh you have to let him write to you – imagine if you ended up getting married...

Walter: Well hold on a minute – what does he want with writing to you? I reckon he
            just said that to get friendly with you. You don't want to give anyone your
            real address anyway – tell him a pretend one or just tell him to sling his
            hook.

Rose: Ha ha, you two are like the angel and the devil on my shoulder! I've
            thought about all of that… and I keep changing my mind! I did say I
            wouldn't get married ever, so as I could keep being a nurse… but this ain't
            marriage anyway, it's just a few letters.

Mary: Did you forget I was going to see this, Rose? You need to be careful here
            love… what if you two find out you get on and then he has to go back out
            and fight? You know better than anyone what can happen to lads out
            there.

Rose: Thanks, Ma. And no, he got a blast right through his right leg, so he won't
            be going back out, ever. It would be nice for him to have someone to write
            to while he's resting up, wouldn't it?

Mary: Well, there's another reason to watch yourself – do you mean they had to
            take his leg off? How would he support you then, if he can't work? I'd steer
            clear of that one if I were you, Rosie.

Rose: They didn't have to take it off – the Germans had already done that for
            him. I don't know. I think I'm going to get some kip and make my mind up
            tomorrow. Oh, and his name's James, but he says to call him Jamie… ain't
            that nice?

9th February

Walter: What happened with the Scottish fellow, Rosie? Did you give him your
            address?

Rose: I did it! Well, I sort of did. I decided to give him my name and where to
            write to me out here, not at home, so if he does write me any letters they'll
            come with the mail like yours do. I wrote it on a scrap of paper and kept it
            up my sleeve for hours, blushing like anything whenever I walked through
            his carriage… and me a thick-skinned nurse! He must've thought I was
            going to give him the cold shoulder. In the end I called Florence over when
            we stopped to take on water (she's another nurse – couldn't help it with a
            name like that, could you?) and told her about it. And she went marching
            right over to his bed and said, "Nurse Carter, come here, you need to take
            a look at this man's vitals…!" Well I thought the ground might as well
            swallow me up. But I went over, didn't have no choice, did I? And I checked
            his pulse, though he could've been stone dead for all I could feel through
            my trembly hands, and just when I was about to walk off I pushed the note
            under his pillow. And now I'm fretting that he won't be able to turn around
            and reach it… but he did give me a wink when I came back through so I
            think he must have got it.

Walter: Blimey, Rose, you sound just like a schoolgirl. Well, at least you didn't give
            him your home address.

Rose:	He probably won't even write, Walt, and it will all be a big fuss about nothing.
Lily:	It is exciting though… did you get to say goodbye?
Mary:	Just you be careful – you could get dismissed for something like that.
Rose:	No, Lil – I was down in another carriage when we got to Boulogne and the orderlies got them off quick. I'll let you know if I get a letter… and Ma, I think it'll be alright – letters don't matter too much, it's just if I went walking out with him, then they'd have something to say!

11th February

Walter:	Well this just goes to show you, don't it? From today's Daily Mirror:

THE BULLDOG AND THE DACHSHUNDS: A STUDY IN TEMPERAMENTS.

These dogs were shown at a dog show yesterday. The British bulldog was characteristically imperturbable, but the German dachshunds exceedingly nervous. They kept looking over their shoulders as though in fear of attacks from behind. It does not transpire whether or not the dachshunds have been naturalised as yet.

12th February

Mary:	I was saying this to you, wasn't I, Ed? Food is so dear… the Express says it's because they've closed the Dardanelles so we can't get nothing from Russia and then so much of our food has to go to the army. They're the 'best fed army ever known'! That's good ain't it? But I've got nothing left over to make leftovers from… Still, I suppose there ain't so many mouths for me to feed now…

WHY FOOD HAS RISEN
IN PRICE.

THE PRIME MINISTER DETAILS
THE CAUSES, BUT HAS
NO REMEDY.

13th February

Walter:	Our boys have carried out an air raid on German bases in Belgium – Bruges, Zeebrugge, Blankenberghe and Ostend! 34 aeroplanes and seaplanes. They bombed railway stations, railway lines and some of the places where they think the enemy are hiding them submarines for the blockade. Well done lads! They didn't actually find any submarines, mind, but the Prime Minister says they're there somewhere.
Lily:	Serves them right after the raid on Great Yarmouth! Somehow I think planes are a bit less creepy than those big Zeppelins though.
Ed:	They're all creepy if they're carrying bombs, aren't they?
Lily:	I suppose so. Anyway, well done boys. Shame about Ostend Station though – I heard it was quite pretty. Poor Belgium has had a rough time of it.
Mary:	The paper says there was no casualties though – very glad to hear it.

15th February

Walter:	Rosie, I've just seen this in the paper. Is it true? I don't know how you can treat a German soldier just like he was a Tommy.

THERE IS NO FAVOURITISM AT A BRITISH HOSPITAL BASE BETWEEN FRIEND AND FOE.

Here, in one of the latest photographs taken at a British hospital base for the wounded in France, are a party of wounded British and German soldiers. Friend and foe receive the same treatment. They lie on the same stretchers, are treated by the same doctors and receive the same care and nourishment. Many of the Germans express great surprise at this treatment. They did not expect it. In the smaller photograph a wounded man is being carried to the base.

Rose:	It's a difficult one, Walt… I feel strange treating them, especially when I think about Charlie, but you have to sometimes. In the base hospitals, if they've got German soldiers in, they'll keep them in a separate room. By and large they get the same care though. Some nurses don't like it, some don't mind it. My friend Florence said that when you're a nurse you can't help but see that we're all just human flesh underneath anyway.

17th February

Walter: What a piece of news we've had! We're moving back to St Albans! Not back with the Abbotts, which is a shame, but where the First Surrey Rifles was staying before – near Holywell Hill. It'll be nice to see the old place again… I'll drop by one day Jane, see how Jimmy and Jack are getting on – I'll bet they've grown a bit since last year!

Fred: It will be nice alright, but I'm that fed up with moving about… we're going to spend the whole war getting trains backwards and forwards from St Albans.

Walter: I don't know Fred, I overheard Captain Wright saying about getting more horses, mules and waggons – now why would they do that if we wasn't planning something?

Fred: Did you? Well I'll believe it when I see it…

Mary: How nice, Walt! Let us know your new address when you can.

Jane: Oh, that's exciting news! Bring Bert as well, won't you. I won't tell the little'uns just yet – they'll be that surprised when you boys walk in!

Walter: I'll look forward to it, Mrs A.

18th February

Mary: I'm so worried about this blockade – it's hard enough getting food as it is, what with the prices.

20th February

| Walter: | Here's some news that will make you feel better Ma – I read today how good our airmen are getting. The Germans don't stand a chance in the Channel with this lot overhead. Take a look at this from the Daily Mirror – 'The remarkable efficiency and development in tactics and daring of our army of the air have been one of the most wonderful features of this almost world war. Two short years ago people stood and stared at a single aeroplane as something which was the latest marvel of science. To-day one fighting fleet alone of forty aircraft is the result of British brains and enterprise.' |

| Mary: | Thanks for this, Walt. I just hope the enemy aren't getting good at it too… I suppose we wouldn't hear about that in the papers. Do you think our boys would be able to see submarines in the sea from up in the air? |

| Walter: | I don't know – I reckon the best way would be to hit their bases, like they tried to do in Belgium. |

| Lily: | I heard some of our pilots only have 5 hours of training before they go up! Sounds terrifying. |

22nd February

| Walter: | I told you, didn't I, Ma! The enemy tried their hand at bombing again and made a right hash of it. They came all the way to Essex to knock down a shed and a cherry tree… I wouldn't worry if I was you. |

THE SKY PIRATES DROP FIRE-BOMBS ON ESSEX TOWNS BUT FAIL TO MURDER EVEN A SINGLE BABY.

24th February

Walter: What a shock with the Indian troops in Singapore! It happened last week
– can't believe we've only just heard about it over here. It was a mutiny –
some men from the 5th Light Infantry rioted. They killed a lot of British
officers and even some civilians. The British and the locals fought back,
and they had help from the Sikhs and some French, Russian and Japanese
sailors… but more than 40 people was killed. I hope it don't happen on the
Western Front now.

John: Hi Walt. Rotten news. The Express says the mutineers were angry about
promotions, but my Pa says it was because the Ottoman Empire is on
Germany's side. The 5th Light Infantry is all Mohammedans see, and
they're fighting for us because they're Indian, but their religion says they
have to do what the Ottoman Sultan says, and he declared a holy war on
Britain last year. So I suppose they had to make a choice.

25th February

Mabel: This is for all you folk who thought the suffragettes was keeping quiet until
the end of the war – 1,000 of them just landed at Le Havre! Two battalions
of 500 women each. They're going to be telephone operators, signallers,
telegraphists and chauffeurs. It's just what Christabel Pankhurst said last
year – women can keep everything running while the men are away. Why
not? Hope it happens over here soon, I'm just about fed up with working at
Arding & Hobbs.

Walter: What do you think about that, Fred? A bunch of women got to Le Havre
before us! That's just about the last straw.

Fred: Blimey, Walt… we'll be the last ones out there at this rate! Still, good on
them – don't know how much good they'll manage to do but they sound
plucky. I like that.

Lily: Oh Arding & Hobbs is alright really, Mabel… besides, you've got me to talk
to. What would you do otherwise anyway?

Mabel: I would miss you Lil, but I wouldn't mind being a chauffeur – I'd like to
drive a motor.

Lily: Now that you mention it, that would be alright wouldn't it? I can just see us
setting off around London!

Fred: Gawd, London's got enough to worry about without you two wreaking
havoc!

26th February

John: The navy has been trying to get up the Dardanelles Strait – Churchill's orders – so we can take Constantinople. This article seems to think they're getting on alright but I don't know – don't our ships look like they're on fire to you? There's rumours coming through that they had a hard time with the Turkish guns and mines.

THE BOMBARDMENT OF THE DARDANELLES: THE FRENCH AND BRITISH FLEETS AT THE ENTRANCE TO THE STRAITS.

THE BOMBARDMENT OF THE DARDANELLES: THE FRENCH AND BRITISH FLEETS AT THE ENTRANCE TO THE STRAITS.

On Friday last the French and British Fleets started bombarding the forts at the entrance to the Dardanelles. A number of Turkish forts were silenced. This remarkable photograph of the Allied fleets at the entrance to the Dardanelles was taken from one of the battleships. It is the intention of the Allies to force the Dardanelles, in which case it is safe to predict that Constantinople will fall into the hands of the Allies.

28th February

Walter: Happy birthday Rose! Hope everything's alright out in France.

Rose: Thanks Walt! It's been alright – I've had an easy day compared to most. It's been sunny weather the past few days so the ground is drying out a bit and we've only got a few men on the train. Mostly measles, diphtheria and some enterics. Florence gave me some fancy soap what her sister had sent her, ain't that nice? Still nothing from Jamie. I don't suppose he'll write after all.

Mary: Good to hear you're having a nice day love – and I'm glad to hear the weather has eased up a bit. Don't give that James fellow a second's thought. I sent up a parcel – did it arrive?

Rose: Thanks, Ma – we've been at Chocques for a few days so I haven't had any post. I'll look forward to picking it up next time we go back!

Walter: I sent you a card as well, Rose – Mrs Abbott told me about a nice stationers on the high street. It is nice being back in St Albans… but I can't help wishing we was out there with you lot.

Rose: Thanks, little brother. And I'm sure it won't be long – they need as many men out here as they can get…

March 1915

1st March

Lily:	Have you seen the Daily Mirror, Mabel? The fashion's coming back from 80 years ago! Big skirts, not them hobble ones no more. Bet we'll see more in the shop. I wish I could afford them! Getting the cut right on a big skirt's easier but it costs a lot more in the material. At least it's a couple of inches off the ground these days, so that saves a bit. I'll see if I can have a go.
Mabel:	I don't know, Lil – it does seem a waste to use all that material when people are trying to save. And to think it was Paris where it started! You'd think the French would know better than anyone that there's a war going on.
Lily:	Well, if I could do it without wasting anything it might be alright... I'm going to see if we have any of Granny's old dresses – maybe I could use the material.

2nd March

Walter:	Did you see the Prime Minister's speech from yesterday? He's been bandying about some numbers that make my head hurt. He says the war so far has cost £362,000,000! I asked one of our Pay Sergeants, Joe, who's good at arithmetic, and if I was still working as a railway porter I'd have to keep going for 7 million years to earn that much! Don't fancy that... Asquith says per day it's £1,500,000 and he reckons it'll be even more than that soon. They've sorted out enough money for 100 more days of war though... so I suppose they don't think it'll be over yet. 100 days from now is June. I hope we get out there before then.
Fred:	It weren't all bad Walt, he said us Territorials are "capable of confronting any troops in the world." Too right we are! They'd better send us out soon...
Mary:	That's good news about the Terriers, Fred. Asquith said he's going to fight back against the blockade too – by blockading Germany. Says they won't let any goods in or out. Hope it makes the enemy see sense.

March 1915

4th March

Walter:	Big news everyone – I reckon we're moving on soon for sure. There's all sorts of kit and equipment arriving and I heard a rumour we're going to the Ypres Salient…
Fred:	I think you're right. You was right about them horses and mules anyway, they're everywhere! New general service and limbered wagons too, and a load of saddles and harnesses.
Mary:	Oh, Walt. Are you really going up near Ypres? I can't bear the thought of it, not after Charlie.
Lily:	That is big news… do you think you'll be going soon? It's been so long since I've seen you, Walt! I had a word with Mrs Reed and I can't get leave from work before the 20th… do you think you'll be going before then?
Walter:	Don't you worry Ma, I'll be alright. And I don't know, Lil – perhaps. I do miss you something rotten. How about we say you'll come to visit on Saturday the 20th (I'll pay for your ticket – I got a bit of extra money with me promotion) and if we're heading off before then I'll let you know.
Lily:	Thank you, sweetheart! Ooh I can't wait! I'll send a message to Haig himself telling him he's not to send for you before then…

6th March

Walter:	The Royal Navy is at it again! They've sunk one of them submarines! Off Dover – U8 it was called. They took the Germans on it prisoner and lined them all up down the pier – I would have liked to have seen that… all the townsfolk came out to see them get marched through the streets in disgrace. Something strange though – the Express said, 'The German officers were to-day the guests of the Royal Artillery officers at lunch at Dover Castle.' Are they being funny? I mean, I wouldn't mind lunch at Dover Castle and I'm fighting on the right side…!
Fred:	That's officers for you, Walt. I can see our own Captain 'Always' Wright getting friendly with the Germans if it meant lunch at Dover Castle.
Walter:	Ha ha, you might be right. They ain't all bad though… who knows, maybe they was getting information out of them? Give them a drop of wine, get them talking…
Fred:	Come on now, don't get all nice about officers now they've made you a Lance Jack.

March 1915

8th March

Walter:	You won't believe what we've just had! A farewell concert in the County Hall! Miss Louise Dale organised it and Madame Ada Crossley was in it too. They weren't half good and they was wishing us luck and saying how brave we all was. Don't know exactly when we're setting off yet, but it must be very soon, mustn't it? We all sang along with 'Keep the Homefires Burning' and I almost got a tear in me eye thinking of you, Lil… Fred got hisself in a right two-and-eight with the drink afterwards though – I nearly had to carry him home! And me almost as bad… I'm going to sleep now.
Lily:	Oh Walt, do you think it'll be before the 20th that you go? I couldn't bear not to see you.
Lily:	Walter?
Walter:	Lil, I'm so sorry, I fell asleep that quick I still had me boots on… I don't know when we're going, sweetheart. I just hope it's not before then. I'll let you know as soon as I find out. Now I've got to go and find some aspirin for me head – except there ain't much around since the war started. Bet Fred could do with some too.

10th March

Walter:	Just to let you know, Ma, and you Lil, some of the 1/23rd are going to be back in Battersea today to deliver the Colours to St Mary's Church. It's so that they'll be safe while we're away. There's going to be the Colour Party and a marching detachment… I wish they'd chosen me for it, then I'd get to see you all. Never mind, eh. Bert will be there, so look out for him. They're starting from Clapham Junction so my old workmates might see them! Let us know if you get out there.
Mary:	We saw them! It was wonderful – they looked ever so smart marching down the road and lots of the young men was able to see their families afterwards. It's hard, really, that only some of you could come.
Lily:	It really was a good sight – we came out of the shop to watch them go by. I pretended that you was there too and cheered and clapped for all I was worth. I do miss you, sweetheart.
Walter:	I miss you and all. Wish I could have been there! But it's good to hear it all went off well. I can just imagine them all setting off past Arding & Hobbs…

11th March

Walter:	How are you getting on, Rose? Heard there's been something doing near a village called… I don't know if I can spell it… Neuve Chapelle?
Rose:	That's it, Walt. The army have been busy up there, which means we'll be busy for the next week or more. We got an emergency call to clear a hospital at Rouen ready for more wounded, so we knew something was up, and now we're being rushed straight back towards the Front again.

<table>
<tr><td></td><td>Not much news about what's actually happening, mind – what are the papers saying back home?</td></tr>
<tr><td>Walter:</td><td>They say it's a 'magnificent offensive action' and we've taken 1,000 prisoners. Sounds alright – maybe you won't have too many of our boys to treat.</td></tr>
<tr><td>John:</td><td>It was the Lahore and Meerut Divisions from our side – they had a good system going with bombardment then infantry. They took Neuve Chapelle itself but it's been blown to bits. The Germans are counter-attacking now though…</td></tr>
</table>

14th March

<table>
<tr><td>Walter:</td><td>Well, do you want the good news or the bad news? Lil, I'm so sorry, but we've had our embarkation orders – we're finally leaving! The 1/23rd is going to get a chance to show Fritz what we're made of. Everyone's in high spirits and there's two trains waiting to take us to Southampton (don't know how I'm going to get comfortable, carrying all me kit, plus me jam sandwiches…) I'm just so sorry it couldn't be after the 20th, Lil, I really am. But you'll write me letters, won't you? Rose says it ain't so far really and the post comes over every day. I don't know much about what it's going to be like really… but we're not going to Ypres after all – they're sending us near Neuve Chapelle instead because of what happened there. Bethune, I think it is. I'm not scared, Ma… well, maybe just a bit. But I can't say I'm not excited too – we've been waiting 8 months for this!</td></tr>
<tr><td>Mary:</td><td>Oh love. I know you've worked so hard for this, but it was always going to be a shock to hear you're actually going… Ed's trying to explain it all to your little sister, bless him, and your father says don't let the sergeants pinch your rum ration. Just keep warm and we'll see you soon, I've no doubt.</td></tr>
<tr><td>Walter:</td><td>Thanks Ma. And Pa. Give Annie a big hug from me too. I'll miss you all (even you, Ed!) but I'll write when I can and it won't be much different from me being up here in St Albans, will it? Do you know if Lil's seen this? Is she alright?</td></tr>
<tr><td>Mabel:</td><td>Walt, you won't believe it – Lily's gone! Herb ran in all out of breath and said he saw her getting on a train at Clapham Junction – we reckon she must have seen your message and set off to Southampton! Her Ma's gone barmy because she's gone off without a chaperone, and Mrs Reed says she'll lose her job. She must really love you, Walt.</td></tr>
<tr><td>Walter:</td><td>Good gawd, has she? Well, we're on our way on the train and I don't know when the ship's leaving! Bless her heart, I'll feel rotten if she loses her job. I hope she makes it – I'm desperate to see her…</td></tr>
<tr><td>Ed:</td><td>You know I don't agree with none of this fighting, but I hope you get on alright. And I hope Lily makes it down. Just keep your wits about you, like your big brothers taught you. Keep safe.</td></tr>
</table>

14th March

Walter: Well, we're on the ship and I ain't seen Lily at all... I been squinting at all the people who've come out to wave us off and I can't see her. I hope she's alright. The lads are having a right laugh at me for getting so worked up about a girl... Lil, I'm on a steam ship called the 'Copenhagen', next to one called the 'Trafford Hall' (the one they're hoisting the horses onto), and I've got me blue handkerchief what you sewed for me and I'm going to wave it about like a lunatic.

Lily: I can see you! I can see you! I'm right at the back, jumping up and down, in me green coat and hat! Can you see me? I'm so sorry I missed you... I'm alright everyone – I'll be back later, I just had to see him. Can you see me, Walt?

Walter: There you are! I see you! You are a one, Lil... I'm glad you're alright. The ship's starting to move, can you get any closer? Me eyesight ain't as good as the army thinks it is...

Lily: Is that better? I'm as close as I can get! I'm going to wave until I can't see you no more... Please look after yourself, Walter. Write to me! I'll see you soon!

Walter: Goodbye, Lil! I wish I could blow you a kiss but the lads would never let me live it down. Oh, to heck with it – here goes... take care sweetheart! And make sure you get home safe. Goodbye everyone!

15th March

Walter: Well, we've arrived at Le Havre! Exactly 7 months after Charlie got here... it was the 15th of August last year that he landed. And now we're here to put things right again. We got off the ship at 8 o'clock this morning and marched to No. 2 Rest Camp – it ain't too far away (3 miles) but we had to march through the town and then up the longest hill you ever seen. Led by the battalion band the whole way though – you should have heard the locals when they started on the Marseillaise! Lots of lovely French girls all smiling and singing. Fred reckons they looks different from English girls somehow… Don't worry though, Lil, they ain't a patch on you! Bless your heart for coming to see me yesterday. Did you get home alright? What did Mrs Reed say?

Mary: Take care of yourself Walter, and you Fred, and let us know how you're getting on whenever you can. Lily got home alright, thank goodness – Mrs Howes was beside herself.

Rose: Welcome to la belle France, Walt! Look after yourself won't you – learn how to make a splint and a tourniquet just in case and you'll be doing yourself a favour.

Lily: I got home alright, thanks sweetheart, but I went to see Mrs Reed and she said to take the day off while she thinks about me job… it was worth it though! Just please be careful out there and don't forget me, will you? I miss you already.

Lily: And I'm sure them French girls ain't so special anyway.

Walter: Thanks Ma, and Rosie I will do. Don't worry though, I'll be alright. And I'd never forget you, Lil! I hope she lets you back – let me know how you get on. It was wonderful to see you… I'll write you a letter when I can.

16th March

Walter: Morning all. The lot of us set off marching at 6.30 this morning… and now we're getting on trains to go to the 'acclimatisation positions' behind the line. I think the place is called 'Ark'? I've got a seat next to Fred, of all the rotten luck… ha ha. I tell you what, these French trains ain't what you'd want to see coming through Clapham Junction… some of the fellows are in carriages like horse boxes and the whole thing moves so bleedin' slow. And I swear I've got lice already – I'm itching all over… It's interesting seeing the countryside as you go by though – people are still working on their farms as if nothing was happening, but every so often you see a little patch of graves… how did it go with your job, Lil?

Fred: Oi! None of your lip! And there's no point looking out the window at graves… I say we start up a round of 'Tipperary' but swap it for 'Clapham Junction'.

Rose: I think you mean 'Arques', little brother.

Lily: It's alright, Walt! She let me back! Mrs Reed's a good sort really. But she says I'm on me last warning and there's to be no more 'man trouble' – not with you or Herb or no one.

Walter: Thank goodness for that! Glad to hear it. Well done. And too right about Herb… alright then, Fred, 'Tipperary', you're on!

17th March

Walter: This made me laugh!

Sketches of a Tommy's life. At the Base – No.8

We left the Base in great style and in cattle trucks. We must have averaged a good mile an hour. The juvenile population along the way make earnest enquiries concerning our iron rations

18th March

Rose: How are you getting on, Walter? We're still busy with all the casualties from Neuve Chapelle… there's been some very bad ones and the train is packed – on Monday I had 120 patients all to myself! Mostly British, and some Canadians, and a lot of Indians too – I heard they captured some of the German line. Some of the poor fellows have been coming through with no dressings on at all though and the Clearing Hospitals are getting 800 at a time. There's bad rumours about mines in the Dardanelles too, but nothing about it in the papers yet…

Mary: Well I'm sure it ain't so bad as Rose is making out, Walter… and it sounds like they'll be glad to have you out there. Keep your spirits up, and no more bad news please, Rose.

Walter: Don't worry – you can keep on telling it like it is Rosie, I can take it. Besides, everything I read says the Allies are advancing, so there must be something doing. We had a rotten journey up to Arques though – arrived at 4 o'clock in the morning after getting on the train at 10 o'clock the morning before… and then we had to find billets in the dark!

20th March

Walter: Well, we have had a miserable time of it. We started on the march to Lespresses yesterday and had to keep on through a blizzard! Sergeant Bridges says it's good practise for working 'under real active service conditions'… We're tough and all (you couldn't not be after all the marching we did in St Albans) but the roads out here has this 'pavé' which is like cobbles. Charlie was right, it ain't half hard on the feet. And he was marching on it in the blistering heat and now here I am in a blizzard. And they say the weather's bad in England! Makes you almost miss some good old Battersea drizzle. I heard some of the French fellows in the Vosges Mountains have been using skis though… now I wouldn't mind that!

Lily: It's snowing here too! Just a little bit though. Your Ma says Mrs Wiggins has bought herself a new fur… I hope you can keep warm enough sweetheart.

23rd March

Mabel: Well, here's a turn up for the books! The government has had a bit of sense about women and work. Ladies, take a look at this notice from the paper and knock for me if you fancy going down the Labour Exchange.

G. R.

WAR SERVICE FOR WOMEN.

The President of the Board of Trade wishes to call attention to the fact that in the present emergency, if the full fighting power of the Nation is to be put forth on the field of battle, the full working power of the Nation must be made available to carry on its essential trades at home. Already in certain important occupations there are not enough men and women to do the work. This shortage will certainly spread to other occupations as more and more men join the fighting forces.

In order to meet both the present and the future needs of national industry during the war, the Government wish to obtain particulars of the women available, with or without previous training, for paid employment. Accordingly, they invite all women who are prepared, if needed, to take paid employment of any kind—industrial, agricultural, clerical, etc.—to enter themselves upon the Register of Women for War Service which is being prepared by the Board of Trade Labour Exchanges.

Any woman living in a town where there is a Labour Exchange can register by going there in person. If she is not near a Labour Exchange she can get a form of registration from the Local Agency of the Unemployment Fund. Forms will also be sent out through a number of women's societies, and can be obtained by post from the General Manager, Board of Trade Labour Exchanges, at the address below.

The object of registration is to find out what reserve force of women's labour, trained or untrained, can be made available if required. As from time to time actual openings for employment present themselves, notice will be given through the Labour Exchanges, with full details as to the nature of work, conditions, and pay, and, so far as special training is necessary, arrangements will, if possible, be made for the purpose.

Any woman who by working helps to release a man or to equip a man for fighting does national war service. Every woman should register who is able and willing to take employment.

Board of Trade, March, 1915.

March 1915

Lily:	That is interesting… I don't know what I'd do though! Talk later?

26th March

Walter:	Brace yourselves – we've had a rumour from the Transport that we might be going into the line tomorrow… Don't know where yet, but maybe Ypres – sounds like it's all getting going up there again. We even had a talk from Field Marshal Sir John French hisself! He said we was all very smart and that they're glad to have Territorials out here now. About bleedin, time I'd say – we've done enough 'bayonet fighting' to last a lifetime now it's time to get stuck in. Wish us luck!
Lily:	Oh sweetheart, best of luck. The thought of it frightens the life out of me.
Mary:	I can't help but wish it weren't Ypres – but you go and give him what for. Your father was glad to hear about Field Marshal Sir John French. Take care love, and make sure Fred's alright too.
Fred:	Thanks, Mrs C!
Ed:	Good luck. Hope you get on alright. Bit of news to keep you going – it was the Grand National today. Remember last year when you won all that money? Well this year Ally Sloper won, ridden by Jack Anthony. Good odds as well – 100/8! I backed a rum one.

27th March

Walter:	What a load of fuss about nothing. The rumour was right – we was supposed to go up to the Ypres Salient, but at the last minute they sent in another bunch of Terriers instead… so we've only moved a bit nearer to the line today, to a place called Labeuvrière. Can hear the guns from here though, and see the lights from the flares, so everyone's excited. Fred even reckons he saw a Taube!
Mary:	They didn't ought to mess you about like that, but I'm glad you ain't going just yet. Oh, and Annie lost one of her baby teeth! She wanted me to post it to you, but I said I didn't think the Tooth Mouse would travel that far. Bless her heart, she still believes that if she throws her tooth behind the grate and a mouse eats it the new one will grow stronger…
Walter:	Ha ha – good girl! Tell her I bet she looks a real beauty with one missing.

29th March

Walter:	Hello everyone. Quick update while I've got a minute. We're busy with training here – learning how to use grenades and that. They're pretty dangerous most of them – handmade and we has to light them with cigarettes. We had a lecture about spying too… did you know they can use pigeons to spy on people? Fred nearly clobbered one poor bird with a grenade that same afternoon. I had to stop him as it didn't look the suspicious type.
Rose:	Thanks for the news – you do make me laugh. I needed something to smile about today… how are you getting on in this wind? It's bitter out here in Sotteville and we've had no heating for a month now!

Walter: It is cold, ain't it? I could do with one of them goatskin coats. Everyone calls them 'Teddy Bears'. Sounds like you could do with one and all. Our camp here ain't so bad, mind – the canvas keeps most of the wind out. Any news from the soldiers about what's happening at the Front?

Rose: Bits and pieces… One fellow who made it out of Neuve Chapelle said because nearly all the stretcher bearers had been hit and there weren't enough motor ambulances, there was wounded soldiers dragging themselves along the road for miles. Says he'll never get the image out of his head.

31st March

Mary: Thought you might like a bit of news from home, Walt – a lot of companies what sound like they've got German names are advertising to remind people that they're British! Look at these – 'Schweppes' and 'Dee and Ess'. I don't know who's got the money to buy 'sparkling water' in the first place, but it's good to know it comes from here all the same.

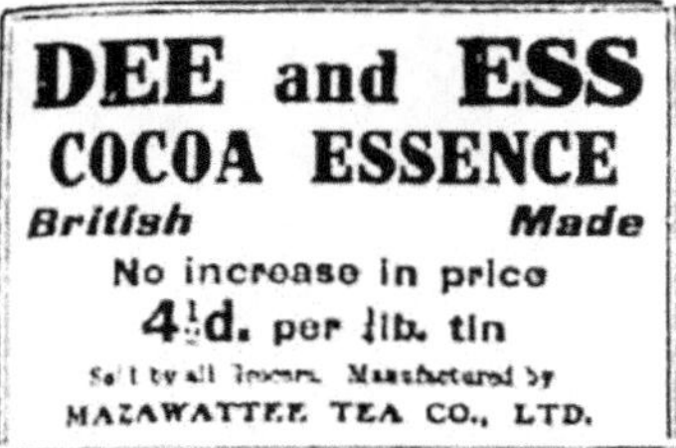

April 1915

<h1 style="text-align:center">April 1915</h1>

1st April

Rose:	I've got some news! I had a letter from Jamie, my Scottish fellow! I'd just about given up hope and then it turned up in the post. It was ever so nicely written. He said he was sorry he hadn't written sooner but he'd had some complications from his amputation. They had to operate again and take it off altogether, at the hip. He's alright now though, no gas gangrene or nothing. Except he has to learn how to do things different. Says it takes a bit of getting used to. Look at this that he said: 'It seems it's easier to destroy than to repair.' Don't he write nicely? He's at the Royal Victoria Military Hospital at Netley – it's just near Southampton so he didn't have too far to go on the train after they got him off the boat. Now I don't know how soon to write back to him… do you think he'll think I'm too keen on him if I write back now?
Walter:	I'm glad he got his act together, I was starting to think he was a rogue. Of course you ought to write back to him, if you want to. If he don't reply, then you'll know he ain't worth the bother.
Rose:	Thanks, Walt, no-nonsense advice as always! How are you getting on yourself?
Walter:	In the pink thanks – we had our first baths in France today! So everyone's feeling chipper again. Let us know what your fellow says if he writes back.
Lily:	Ooh that's good, Rose! Did he say anything nice? And good news on the baths, Walter! I don't know if I could go two weeks or more without a bath… even when I don't want to carry all the water over from the copper I go down the public baths.
Rose:	Oh he was very nice in his letter, Lily. Seems he liked my curls, of all things! If he didn't mind me all grubby from nursing then if he ever sees me 'after the war' he'll think I'm Mary Pickford!

2nd April

Walter:	Good Friday today. The Bishop of London held a service that got everyone all stirred up – you should have heard him – he reckons this is a holy war and that we're putting our lives on the line for 'freedom, honour and chivalry' just like Christ did. Now, I ain't been much of a church-going man in me life but I had a word with our padre, Captain Barley, about it afterwards. He's alright, old Barley. His job is to talk to us if we get worried out here and he does services too – on Sundays as normal, but he says he'll do them before battle and at burials as well… He said to me he mostly agrees with what the Bishop said, but he don't want anyone to give their life if they can help it – even Germans. He reckons God has to be on our side though because we're the protectors, looking out for little Belgium. I hope he's right.
Fred:	Of course he's right! I like our Charlie Barley. Whenever he says anything serious he always has this look like he'd rather be having a joke with you. I could tell he weren't too keen on that Bishop though – I reckon he thought

he was a bit fierce with all that business about killing – 'to kill Germans; to kill them, not for the sake of killing, but to save the world; to kill the good as well as the bad, to kill the young as well as the old, to kill those who have shown kindness to our wounded...'

6th April

Walter: Hope everyone had a good Easter! Rumours are getting going again here, about us going into the line... don't know if we should believe it now, after last time. Either way, I hope they still plan on giving us a rum ration – we heard about the King and his household giving up booze for the whole of the war! And Kitchener too. They say it's because there's not enough munitions being made and if people didn't get drunk they could make a lot more. Don't know about that... I do know that anyone who says you don't need a bit of drink from time to time ain't never had to sleep outside.

NO. 4,674.   LONDON, THURSDAY, APRIL 1, 1915.   ONE HALFPENNY.

THE KING ON DRINK: HIS OFFER.

Buckingham Palace, March 30, 1915.

Dear Chancellor of the Exchequer,—The King thanks you for so promptly letting him have a full report of the proceedings at yesterday's meeting of the deputation of employers.

His Majesty has read it with interest, but also with the deepest concern. He feels that nothing but the most vigorous measures will successfully cope with the grave situation now existing in our armament factories.

We have before us the statements, not merely of the employers, but of the Admiralty and War Office officials responsible for the supply of munitions of war, for the transport of troops, their food and ammunition.

From this evidence it is without doubt largely due to drink that we are unable to secure the output of war material indispensable to meet the requirements of our army in the field, and that there has been such serious delay in the conveyance of the necessary reinforcements and supplies to aid our gallant troops at the front.

The continuance of such a state of things must inevitably result in the prolongation of the horrors and burdens of this terrible war.

I am to add that, if it be deemed advisable, the King will be prepared to set the example by giving up all alcoholic liquor himself and issuing orders against its consumption in the Royal Household, so that no difference shall be made, so far as his Majesty is concerned, between the treatment of rich and poor in this question.—Yours very truly,

STAMFORDHAM.

The Right Hon. D. Lloyd George, M.P., Chancellor of the Exchequer.

Fred: They'd better not take away our booze! Gawd, there'd be a mutiny.

Bert: It's that David Lloyd George, ain't it? The Chancellor. Wants to stop people drinking altogether. If they stop our rum ration, I'm quitting...

9th April

Walter: Moved closer to the line so getting very near the fighting now... Just had a kit inspection. Laid out everything on a groundsheet and Sergeant Bridges came round first to check everything was present and correct (so Lt Summers, our Platoon Commander, wouldn't give him a hard time). We got on alright – most of our things was only replaced the other day anyway – our old leather 1903 kit got swapped for the standard issue 1908 web version. It's a lot better as it's got the right sized pouches for the Lee Enfield Rifle ammunition clips. We has to carry a lot of stuff – rifle, ammunition, bayonet, entrenching tool, blankets, spare boots, housewife (that's a sewing kit), shaving kit, greatcoat, rations, a large pack and a small pack... it's a wonder we can move at all.

11th April

Walter: What a day we've had today… a long march to the reserve line with all our kit, then waiting there until it got dark before we could move forward. The reserve line weren't like what I'd imagined – just a few ruined farm buildings, full of fellows who'd just come from the trenches. They didn't look too sharp if I'm honest, with head to toe mud and looking dead beat. The Sgt Major would have had our guts for garters if we'd showed up looking like that… then as soon as it got dark, two guides came to lead us to the front line trench. We had to go single file – no fags, no talking. There was a slope at the entrance and we landed in about a foot of cold water at the bottom. That's when I realised none of this is like what we thought it would be. From what I could see, it looked like they couldn't dig down no more because of the wet, so they built up instead – the front of the trench was all sandbags and timbers, about 6ft tall. And the trench itself is only wide enough for about 3 men to stand shoulder to shoulder. There's a smell too a real rotten smell. I didn't ask what it is.

Lily: Oh, I hate the idea of you being in a trench. I hope it's quiet and you ain't in too much danger. Is there really a foot of cold water in the bottom of it? It sounds rotten.

Mary: You sound very tired, love. Try and find yourself a dry place to sleep and I'm sure everything will look better in the morning. Take care of yourself.

12th April

Walter: Seems we're really in the thick of it now. We ain't got too much cover, because of not being able to dig… and no communication trenches, so almost everything has to be done in view of the enemy. Two of our fellows got wounded by snipers just this afternoon – we heard the call for stretcher bearers go up… first time I've heard that. They weren't my Section, but I heard Bridges saying one of them, a chap called Barden, didn't look too good. We've had shells bursting all over too – it is a sight – we was all gawping at them exploding on the supply routes at the rear until we got an earful off the fellows we've been stationed with. We've been put with the

1st Guards Brigade to show us how to get on out here. They're good lads. And they had a point about the shells – I reckon one could really smash a man up. Trouble is, it seems we don't have hardly any shells to fire back with… I suppose this is what they mean by the shell shortage…

THE MYSTERY OF THE SHELL SHORTAGE.

Mary: It sounds awful out there – I do hope you're keeping ok… Now I know you have more important things on your mind, but just to remind you, it's Annie's birthday today. Don't worry, I told her you'd wished her a 'Happy Birthday'.

Walter: Oh, I forgot! Rotten brother I am. Everything's just so new out here Ma – half the time I don't know what day it is. Thanks for telling her that… poor kid. Give her a hug from me and tell her I bet she looks 9 years old, not 8.

15th April

Walter: Bad news today – one of the chaps that got hit, that Barden from C Company… he didn't make it. They buried him yesterday, at Richebourg. We didn't see the ceremony, only the band went along as bearers. They said the padre made a good job of it. Don't like to think about it too much – Cpl Dart says it just happens and you has to get on with it. I suppose he's right. And then we heard there's been Zeppelin raids back home… glad no one was killed. Is everyone alright, Ma?

Mary: Good to hear from you and we're sorry to hear about your pal. We're alright thank you and none of them rotten Zeppelins has been by – they was up at Tyneside, not round here… It is getting a bit of a trial to buy food though. It's the cost of bread – 8 ½ pence for a quarter loaf! You remember it used to be 5 ½? I don't know how I'll feed us all if it carries on the same.

Walter: That sounds rotten… can you still get enough grub for everyone, just about? It's been in the papers so maybe Asquith will do something about it.

Mary: You mustn't worry yourself about it son, I'm sorry I mentioned it. We're getting by just fine and I'm sure we have more to eat than you boys do.

16th April

Rose: Sorry to hear you lost one of your chaps, Walt. I saw a burial today – stopped and watched because it was a British soldier. Other nurses see them all the time at the Base Hospitals but we don't so much, being on the trains. It was something alright – they had a Union Flag over the coffin, which was just a thin wooden box really, and a firing party and everything. The padre read – about a hundred men was there listening… and all of a sudden I thought of all of those fellows I've tried to help, the ones who didn't make it and even the ones who did, and I couldn't help it, I cried my heart out for every one of them. The tears don't hardly come when you're working – you can't let them – and after a while you just toughen up to it. But that funeral really did for me. It's funny, they dig the graves very close together in these military cemeteries – I suppose they have lots to fit in. Each one gets a cross to mark it though. Anyway, I hope you're alright, Walt – I've been hearing all sorts of guns and crashes up here. Sounds like things are getting busy again. The star shells are the worst (the ones that look like fireworks). They're miles away, and I know they're meant to light everything up, but all the same they're rotten for keeping you awake at night… I could do with a good night's sleep, I really could.

17th April

Walter: Woke up full of aches and pains this morning – that's always the way first thing, what with being outside and getting half frozen. And no one hardly gets any sleep anyway, even if you ain't on sentry – the war don't stop overnight, so you just has to sleep anywhere you can, whatever time of day or night it is. Still, everyone has to be awake for 'Stand To' just before dawn and at last light. That's when we has to get all our equipment on and take up a 'firing position' against the front of the trench – rifles and bayonets pointed towards the German lines. It's for protection, really – they reckon you're more likely to get attacked at dawn or dusk, so we takes precautions. Our first 'Stand To' was when I got me first proper look at 'No Man's Land', the bit between us and the enemy. That was a shock. They've got bodies still lying out there from who knows when. And rats all picking at them. It makes me feel sick thinking about it. Then we have breakfast whenever we can and get on with the fatigues of the day – mostly fixing up the trench and digging channels to drain the water. Just heard from Jonnie Dart that the Brits took Hill 60 back… That's good. Hope they can hold onto it.

<h1 style="text-align:center">April 1915</h1>

20th April

Walter:	Well, we're out of the trenches – billeted at Allouagne. Can't believe it's only a week or so ago that we went in… I feel like a different man altogether. Learnt a lot from the veterans but we're all just exhausted. We do have a laugh some of the time, but mostly it's bloody awful. There was that many snipers out there and in some places all we had for protection was canvas screens so they couldn't see us so easy. Another fellow got hit – Private Drury. They buried him yesterday. I suppose two killed ain't so many… but it shakes you up. Donald, one of the lads from the Black Watch, said we was lucky it weren't more, what with everyone sticking their heads up when they shouldn't.
Mary:	Walter Carter, you watch your language. I'm glad you're out of the firing line though, son. Let us know how you get on.
Walter:	I'm sorry Ma, it's just you get used to it with all the lads out here… they've got some foul mouths on them! And it helps somehow, when you're having a tricky time. I learnt some words I never even heard on the railways…
Mary:	Well you just keep them to yourselves, I won't have you coming back home talking like a ruffian.
Walter:	Don't worry, once I get home it'll be just like old times, you'll see…

22nd April

Walter:	Marched to Auchel today for a bath. About bleedin, time. It's funny, everyone ends up looking white as a sheet from the dried mud – clothes and boots and faces and all… got some nice billets now though and I'm even learning some of the French lingo, like you did Rose! 'Napoo' – that means there ain't none left, 'toot sweet' means do it quick and a 'poilu' is a hairy French soldier!
Rose:	Ha ha, oh Walt that's not French! That's just what you soldiers say instead of the real words… one of the sisters I work with comes from a very well-to-do family and she's been doing a few lessons on the side, teaching us all to speak French proper. 'Napoo' is really 'il n'y en a plus' and 'toot sweet' is 'tout de suite'… I think 'poilu' is right though, and you've got the meanings spot on.

23rd April

Walter:	Rotten news this morning. Sergeant Bridges told us the Germans used poisonous gas as a weapon, up on the Ypres Salient. Yesterday evening it was. Nasty stuff – no one knew what it was, just this cloud of something coming over towards them, smelling like pineapple and pepper. It was the French and Algerian soldiers (the ones they call the Zouaves) that got the worst of it. Some of them tried to outrun it, some stayed because they didn't know what the orders was, and then they all started choking on it. I don't like to say too much about what they reckon it does to you… it don't sound nice. A load of fellows died and the rest need hospital treatment. Trouble was, it left a great gap in the line and the Germans broke through

and started heading towards Ypres itself. The Canadians up there have been putting up a good defence and the French tried a counter attack but still it don't look good. This ain't what I thought war would be like at all. I'm glad we're out of the line.

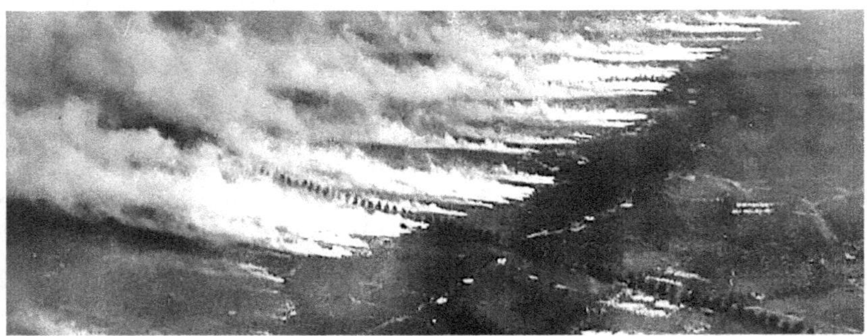

Lily: I'm glad you're out of it too! It sounds rotten. We ain't heard nothing about it here – the papers are just full of news about umarried mothers having 'war babies'. They're wondering what women should do about it and whether we ought to treat these mothers kinder than normal because their fellows are soldiers.

Mabel: What women should do about it? Ain't it got nothing to do with the men then? I've heard it takes two…

Mary: Oh love, that gas sounds evil. Here's hoping there's no more of it… I hope we can hang on at Ypres too.

25th April

Rose: I've been moved! No more jolting about on hospital trains, I've been sent nearer to the line to be part of a 'Field Ambulance'. Now, a Field Ambulance ain't a vehicle – it's a unit of the Royal Army Medical Corps, made up of all sorts of medical officers and nurses and orderlies and we treat soldiers quite close to the action… my pal Florence said we're now 'at the back of the front'! She's a clever one. Anyway it's all go already with this gas-fumes business – the medical staff here have been doing experiments in a barn to try and find a way to stop it. They keep going in and out with masks soaked in different antidotes… I don't know how well any of it's working though and they've all got rotten coughs now. One fellow had too much chlorine and couldn't breathe so we had to give him fumes of ammonia until he felt better.

Walter: Well, at least they're working on it! Makes me feel a bit better. We're back in the line now –not much doing but you still got to be careful of snipers and mortars. We've had a couple of fellows wounded.

Rose: Sorry to hear it, Walt – I hope they pull through. Good news here though – our chaps in the barn have figured out something to put over their mouths so they can go and help anyone caught in this gas without suffering themselves! They do work quick.

FOUL FIGHTING BY THE GERMANS.

OUR ALLIES DRIVEN BACK BY NEW APPLIANCES THAT EMIT ASPHYXIATING GASES.

28th April

Walter: It's another sunny day – Fred's been going about saying it's as hot as summer! And it seems there's something doing everywhere except here… They're fighting around Ypres still and they say the enemy made it over the Yser canal… everyone reckons they're heading for Dunkirk. Wish we could have a go at them as I get angry thinking about them getting that far. And then our chaps from Australia, New Zealand and home, plus the French, have landed on either side of the Dardanelles Strait, out at the Gallipoli peninsula… hope it's going alright for them – Corporal Dart reckons the terrain is tricky out that way. Got to go – just heard we're getting relieved by the 24th Londons. They're South London Terriers too, from the drill hall in Kennington.

30th April

Walter: Well, I ain't never known a day like today! We've had a few working parties go out recently… that's where you has to go out in a group to do things like road building or fetching up wire and ammunition… and today I was picked for one! There was 2 officers and 100 of us men, and we marched to the 'Indian Village', up by Richebourg-l'Avoue. They calls it the 'Indian Village' because the Meerut Division of the Indian Army is there and they has all the special ways of doing their food properly and places where they can pray. Glad they've got that now – at the start of the war no one really thought about what they might need to eat. It was quite a shock going there if I'm honest… I mean, you do get people from different countries in Battersea but I ain't never seen an Indian soldier before… it's just like you said, Rose, they has these turbans to keep their hair in. Some of them speak a bit of English, mind. I had a word with a fellow called Sidh who said the winter's been very hard for them. They come from a hot climate see and they didn't have all the gear to keep warm. He said he volunteered when he saw a poster that said there'd be 'lots of rest, lots of respect, very little danger and a good salary'… but he's written home since to say it ain't like that.

May 1915

1st May

Ed: This is what going to war gets you – more expensive beer. It ain't bleedin, fair. I don't want to fight, I just want to do me work and have a beer at the end of the day. Simple. And I know you been saying you need more shells to blast the other fellow with, Walt, but taxing drink to get the money for them is just a shifty way of trying to get everyone teetotal.

TAXING DRINK TO SECURE SHELLS.

MR. LLOYD GEORGE'S SWEEPING PROPOSALS TO MAKE MEN SOBER.

PRICES UP ALL ROUND.

3rd May

Walter: Just heard we're going back into the line to relieve the 24th Londons… not looking forward to it. Lot of to-ing and fro-ing, this war. Me and Fred was in a working party at Chocolat Menier Corner today – the army comes up with all sorts of names for places, so we know where we are. We've learnt where 'Orchard Communication Trench' is, and 'Bomb House'… the mob what was here before us named them. Anyway, this bit was called 'Chocolat Menier Corner' because there's a sign up for a French chocolate company.

4th May

Walter:	Just had the biggest scare I've ever had – my heart's beating so hard I swear I can hear it. I was ordered to take the lads from my section to fix up the wire about 30 feet in front of our trench – would be right in view of the German line if it weren't dark. Nasty stuff, barbed wire. It's meant to stop the enemy getting to our trench but it's a devil to uncoil and hang on the posts and it's easy to catch yourself on it if you're not careful. Anyway, we had our sentries out and was working away when suddenly Fritz sent up a flare. Honest, it was just like daylight. We all dropped to the ground but Tommy Mills was just a bit too slow, got hit by a sniper and fell onto the wire. We managed to pull him down and as soon as the flare died out I shouted to the boys to make a run for it. Me and Bert somehow got Tommy back to the trench between us but I could hear bullets whizzing past me ears all the while. Heaven knows how we all got back in one piece… I've never been so glad to see the right side of the parapet. Looked around for Fred after we all fell into the trench and felt sick when I couldn't see him, thinking I'd just scarpered and left him behind. But he came leaping in just after me, white as a sheet and with his tunic ripped up. Someone get us some hot tea, I'm shaking like a leaf.
Fred:	Rum, more like! I caught me sleeve on a bit of wire when we dropped down. Thought that would've done for me but I got it free in the end. I'll have to get me 'housewife' out. Glad you and Bert got back alright. I saw the stretcher bearers carrying Tommy Mills off to the Regimental Aid Post… if I'm honest, he didn't look too good. And don't worry about waiting for me old pal, just get yourself to safety if something like that happens.
Walter:	I know Fred, but I promised Ma I'd look after you… still, fat lot of use it'd be looking out for you if you're going to use our own barbed wire to trap yourself!
Fred:	Ha, fair point – bit of an own goal wasn't it? Gawd I need that rum.
Lily:	Oh Walt, that could have been the end of you! It makes my stomach turn to think of it. I can't help it, I keep hoping maybe you could get just a little injury so you could come home… the headline in the paper the other day was 'Wounded on Friday, home in England by Sunday, watching the Chester races on Wednesday'! Here, look:

They all enjoyed the day's sport.

6th May

Walter:	We've been given 'anti-gas appliances'! There's not much to them but here's hoping they'll help. We've got a cotton wool pad each, covered in black gauze – it goes over your nose and mouth, with elastic round your head, and if the gas comes you soak it in carbonate of soda. Bridges says the 'ammonia' will 'neutralise' the gas. I don't understand what he says half the time. But he did say if you don't have no carbonate of soda then you just… well, you has to 'urinate' on them, and that has ammonia in just the same. Sorry, Ma.
Fred:	I've never had so much trouble not laughing as when he told us that! He was that serious about it, and there was me trying not to catch your eye Walt! Thought I was going to burst…
Rose:	You'll be glad of it if you need to use it! I've seen some fellows with gas poisoning now I'm closer to the line, and there's a fair few Canadians who would've been a lot worse off if they hadn't known that trick. The Express says the Allies might start using gas as well… 'As we have to kill some seven to eight millions of Germans before the war ends, I think this English gas should be used as soon as convenient to ourselves.' Worrying when they put it like that…

REPRISALS FOR POISON GAS?

BRITISH INVENTION READY FOR USE.

To the Editor of the " Daily Express."

Sir,—It is twenty-four years ago since a British admiral invented a gas " which would end all war in twenty-four hours or so." The Germans heard of the invention and themselves proposed the resolution prohibiting the use of asphyxiating gases, at The Hague Convention. The invention was duly pigeon-holed at the War Office.

As we have to kill some seven to eight millions of Germans (territory seems not to be in issue) before the war ends, I think this English gas should be used as soon as convenient to ourselves.

F. J. MATHEWS.
Law Society's Hall, W.C.

8th May

Mary: I don't know how much news you get out there, Walt, but I thought you should see this from the paper. Yesterday the Germans sunk a passenger liner that had come over from New York – there was 1,978 people on board, poor souls… it's like the Titanic all over again. The Americans ain't got nothing to do with this war but I wouldn't be surprised if this made them want to join in.

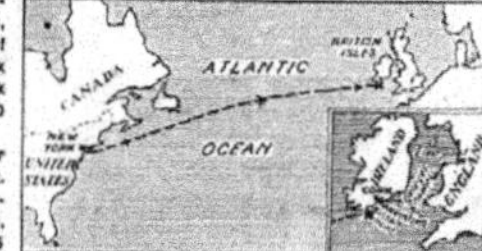

LUSITANIA TORPEDOED & SUNK IN EIGHT MINUTES.

German piracy reached its climax yesterday when the great Cunard liner Lusitania, with 1,978 souls on board, was sunk without warning by a submarine twenty-three miles west of Queenstown.

Up to a late hour last night only the scantiest details of the outrage had been received in London. Between 500 and 600 survivors, many of whom were injured and were taken to hospital, were landed last night at Queenstown. Some others have been landed at Kinsale. As the liner sank eight minutes after she was torpedoed there may have been considerable loss of life. Many prominent persons had booked passages in the Lusitania, including Mr. Charles Frohman, Mr. Alfred Vanderbilt, Mr. D. A. Thomas, Sir Hugh Lane, Lady Mackworth, and Lady Allan, wife of Sir Hugh Allan, of Montreal.

While the incident may impress the imagination by reason of the size of the liner, it will in no degree impair the courage of the nation, and will not have the slightest effect on the course of the war. It is simply an act of piracy and nothing more.

The Lusitania left New York on Saturday last with passengers and mails for Liverpool. Just before she sailed the German Embassy, on instructions from Berlin, published in the New York newspapers a warning to travellers that they embarked in British liners at their own risk. Anonymous warnings were also sent to persons who had booked berths, but little attention was paid to these communications, and the number of passengers created a record for the time of the year. There were on board:—First Class Passengers, 290 ; Second Class Passengers, 662 ; Third Class Passengers, 361 ; Crew, 665. Total, 1,978.

The first indication that the Germans might attempt to carry their threat into effect was afforded on Thursday afternoon by the presence of an enemy submarine in Dunmanus Bay, next to Bantry Bay, on the south-west coast of County Cork and eighty miles west of Queenstown. The submarine came close to the shore, and, having manoeuvred on the surface for some time, dived and was not seen again. Rumours were current in the City yesterday afternoon that the Lusitania had been attacked, and at 5.30 the Admiralty announced that she had been torpedoed and sunk off the Head of Kinsale, south of County Cork. Soon after the news became known in London the offices of the Cunard Company in Cockspur-street were besieged by friends of passengers, including many Americans, and expressions of indignation were heard on every hand. In New York the news caused intense excitement, and the stock market collapsed, all stocks falling from 5 to 10 points.

During the day it became known that two other large Liverpool steamers had been sunk in St. George's Channel on Thursday by German submarines. They were the Candidate, of 5,856 tons, bound for Jamaica, and the Centurion, of 5,945 tons, bound for Durban.

CAPTAIN TURNER, The Lusitania's Commander.

MAP SHOWING THE SCENE OF THE DISASTER.

10th May 1915

Walter: We're out of the line for the next few days, back in billets… it didn't start off too restful, mind – had to get up at 3 o'clock in the morning and Stand To on the parade ground until a quarter past 5! Then the rest of the day is having a bath in the canal and handing all our winter blankets back in to the Quartermaster's Stores – it's warm enough not to need them now. I'm struggling with all the paperwork for it but at least it keeps me mind off Charlie – it would have been his 30th birthday today. I miss him. I keep wishing I could ask him all sorts of things like how to get by out here and how not to get scared by it all. Hope you're all getting on alright at home… is Annie alright?

Mary: Morning, love. Yes it's a hard day… it breaks my heart to think about him. I hope the lads out there can cheer you up a bit. I helped Annie light a candle for him. She's not doing too bad. Your father's gone quiet. No change there. Take care – I'm glad you're out of the line today.

Ed: Well, you know how I feel about it – he shouldn't never have been killed in the first place… but let's keep our chins up, eh? Charlie wouldn't have wanted us moping around.

Rose: Hello all. It's rotten feeling this sad all over again… still, it gives us a nice reason to think about him, doesn't it? Hopefully next year we can all be together for his birthday – just everyone try and keep safe in the meantime won't you.

13th May

Walter: I was going to write and tell you all about how our division is changing
its title to 47th (London) Division, but then we got the news from back
home... are you lot in London alright? Heard about the rioting – people
looting shops and that. Are you alright Lil? Did they get to Arding &
Hobbs?

Lily: Hello, sweetheart. We're alright, don't worry – it's just shops owned by
Germans that they're going for. We closed up early though and (don't
get cross) Herb walked me home because there was some trouble around
Clapham Junction – not nearly as bad as the East End, mind. There weren't
enough policemen and mobs were stealing all the stock and setting fire
to some of the buildings... it's been happening in other big cities too –
Liverpool and Sheffield. They'd already been boycotting the shops but this
is the worst it's been yet.

MOBS LOOT ALIENS' SHOPS IN THE EAST END.

Walter: It sounds rotten... I'm glad you're alright. What's all this about Herb
walking you home though? That ain't his place. I'm glad you had someone
to keep you safe, but couldn't you and Mabel go together? Or maybe Ed
could meet you or something?

Lily: Oh it's alright. After I rushed off down Southampton to see you go, he's
left off saying anything about love and that – he's just... around. You ain't
got no need to worry.

14th May

Walter: I heard some of the German papers are doing cartoons about our fellows
who got murdered with that rotten gas... I don't see how it's funny.

Ed: It's rotten taste, but we been doing cartoons that make fun too... I saw this postcard of the Kaiser for sale the other day – made me laugh.

May 16th

Lily: I wondered why all those men was sitting around outside the station with cases! The government is putting German nationals in 'internment camps' while the war's on. They say it's for their own safety as much as anything, after the riots... it's only the men, mind – women and children and anyone over 55 is being sent back to Germany. I don't know if they ought to split up families like that, but I suppose they had to do something.

ALIENS' MOVING DAY: DRIVEN TO INTERNMENT CAMP IN FURNITURE VANS.

20th May

Walter:	Something's up, I'm sure of it. A bunch of our officers went off to visit a busy part of the trenches today (three of them got concussion from a shell blast while they was there and all) – I'm not allowed to tell you where. Makes us all think they might be planning something big… please don't worry too much, it might not be for a few days yet, or it might not even happen.
Mary:	You do know how to worry your mother…it makes me sick with fright to think of you in so much danger. I know you have to watch what you say in case the enemy gets wind of it, but it would be a comfort to at least know where you are.
Walter:	Sorry, Ma… like I said, it probably won't happen yet, or at all. I'll let you know. Word is our artillery have already started trying to break up their barbed wire though – they do that so we could get through if we did go over. I can't say no more. Tell Lily, um… tell Lily that I love her.
Lily:	Walter Henry Carter, I love you too. Sweetheart, it's the most rotten, rotten feeling not knowing what's going on. Still, I reckon you're one of the best there – you'll be alright, won't you?

21st May

Walter:	Just time to write. Billeted in local town but shelled this afternoon. Lots wounded, one killed. I'm alright, so is Fred. Knock to the head but alright. Can't understand why locals don't leave. Their only home I suppose. Write more when I can.

Lily:	I'm so glad you're alright! And poor Fred – I hope it weren't to bad. The locals must be made of tough stuff

22nd May

Mary:	I know you ain't got much time to spare, Walt, but just passing on this news. Such an awful thing – and Territorials too…

TROOP TRAIN DISASTER.

168 PERSONS KILLED AND 230 INJURED NEAR CARLISLE.

THE KING'S MESSAGE.

VICTIMS IN BLAZING WRECKAGE.

The most terrible disaster in the history of British railways occurred on Saturday ten miles north of Carlisle.

It is impossible yet to ascertain the total casualties, but it is feared that the figures are at least as follows :—

KILLED 168
INJURED 230

Of the killed all but six were men of the 7th Territorial Battalion of the Royal Scots, and nearly all the injured also belong to that battalion.

Walter: That's terrible... I wonder what caused it? Heaven knows we could've done with them out here, especially with what we have to do this week.

24th May

Walter: Back in the line to relieve exhausted 22nd London Regiment. Already lost men just entering trenches. Artillery knocking seven bells out of the enemy though. Reckon we'll soon be going over. Can't write more.

Lily: I know you're not allowed to say nothing more but we're thinking of you. Your Ma's worried. Keep in touch.

25th May

Walter: It's time – we're going over. Plan is to run across and take the German trench on the other side. Two platoons have just gone ahead and we're waiting for the order to follow. Standing in our trench, all next to each other with bayonets ready, quiet. Got our share of rum. More than normal. The guns are getting going now – Fritz must have realised what's happening. Awful screams from No Man's Land. Don't think about it. 30 second warning. When you hear the whistle you just got to go. Charlie, brother, this is for you...

Mary:	Oh heavens. God bless him, keep him out of harm.
Lily:	Oh it's horrible. Good luck, sweetheart. They must have got over by now? He said it's only 200 yards to the enemy trench. I hope he's got through alright… let us know soon as you can, Walt – I can't sit still until I know you're alright.
Rose:	Just got to pray the odds are on his side – they reckon it's one in ten who get killed in an offensive. He'll be alright. Let us know as soon as you can.

26th May

Mary:	Please let us know if you're alright love, we're worried sick…

27th May

Walter:	I'm still in one piece everyone. Well, just about. So damn tired. We did it though, we took the trench… Trench J.7 it was, at Givenchy. Sorry I couldn't tell you before. We've had a bloody awful time of it. We heard the whistle go and I don't even remember what I did – must have got up the ladder and over the top somehow. Then we was running. We got the worst of it. The two platoons that went first mostly got through before the guns started up, but by the time we got up Fritz had realised what was what and gave us hell for it. Getting across the ground weren't easy neither. Nearly lost me footing in a few shell holes and had to dodge fellows who'd already gone down. One shouted to me for help but I didn't stop. Couldn't have stopped. I think I saw a French soldier who must have been laying out there for months. Most god-awful thing I ever seen.

Then, I realised Cpl Dart weren't next to me no more and I panicked and thought, 'does that mean I'm in charge now?' And suddenly we was at the German trench – well, it weren't hardly a trench no more – our artillery had smashed it all up before we got there and we couldn't even get in it. We each had two empty sandbags with us and had to try to fill them with dirt and make some sort of defence. Two measly sandbags against them big German guns firing at us from the side. Maurice Galloway from the signals section did a grand job – ran a telephone wire out to our position, so we was in touch across No Man's Land within 3 minutes. The enemy kept cutting the line with shells though so he had to keep redoing it. They got him in the end, poor lad. And Sergeant Oxman saved a lot of us by building traverses… that's where you build up the trench walls so they're not a straight line – means enemy fire can't travel so far.

The First Surrey Rifles dug communication trenches and our machine guns got up to us just before midnight, but our howitzers couldn't smash the German guns until daybreak. Don't know how I stayed alive that long. Didn't see one German soldier though. Not a live one, that is. Anyway, we held the trench all day under awful fire and the 20th Londons took over at 4pm. We're back behind the line in billets now, but… oh god it's awful… Jonnie Dart's gone, Bert said he saw him go down. And the worst thing is… I can't find Fred. Not nowhere. No one saw him hit, or maybe they just don't want to tell me… but he ain't here. I'm so sorry.

Mary: Oh love, I don't know what to say. I'm so relieved you're alright, but what awful news about dear, dear Fred. Keep your chin up – is there a chance he might turn up yet?

Lily: I can't tell you how glad I was to see your message – I went running to tell my Ma. But oh poor Fred. I'm going to go round Mabel's – I don't know if you know, but she had a soft spot for him. Please let us know if you hear anything.

28th May

Walter: No news about Fred yet… 122 men have been buried so far but no mention of him. They reckon we lost more than 200 men in that offensive, just from our battalion. And another 250 or so injured. They've had to make our whole battalion into 2 companies, not 4, because there ain't enough men no more. I'm in No.1 Company now. Colonel Streatfeild reckons the reason we lost so many is because we didn't have enough shells… he says it might get better now that Lloyd George is Minister of Munitions. Anyway, we got given this from the newspaper – looks like we're doing alright after all.

Reverend: I'll be holding a service later, Walter. And I'm always around to talk – I'm missing Fred myself. Let me know if you'd like a quiet word.

Walter: Thanks. I might.

30th May

Walter: You won't believe it! Guess who just walked in? Only Fred! He's alive but he ain't well. Poor chap ain't saying much and looks to have lost about two stone. He's been sent to see the Medical Officer. I asked where he'd been but he just said he got 'held up'. We've had a few men turn up over the past few days but I was giving up hope that Fred might be one of them. I hope he's alright. I'm made up that he's back.

Mary: Oh what good news! Do you know, I had a feeling he was alright. They'll have him back to normal in no time, I'm sure

Mabel: Thank Heaven. Do you think he'll be alright Walt? I'm going to write him a letter – can you let us know where you are?

Walter: Thanks, Mabel – just put 1206 Pte Dickenson F, 23rd Bn the London Regt, BEF. Like the letters Lil writes to me.

Lily: Wonderful news! Poor dear Fred, I wonder what happened to him?

Rose: So glad to hear about Fred. Give him time – it sounds like he's been through it a bit.

June 1915

1st June

Mary: What a palaver last night! Boy Scouts with bugles and policemen with their whistles cycling up and down shouting "Take cover!" Ed went out to see what was what and they told him them awful Zeppelins was coming. Well it was 11 o'clock at night so we didn't know what to do. Annie woke up with all the noise and wanted to watch out the window, daft thing. In the end we all brought our blankets and slept downstairs. All four of us with our heads under the table! What a sight. Luckily they didn't get down this way. I hope no one was hurt. Looks like the papers are having to watch themselves when they write about it though, so they don't give nothing away to the enemy. 'The Times' is already in trouble…

FOR THE PUBLIC SAFETY.

We received the following official communication early this morning:—

The Press are specially reminded that NO statement whatever may be published dealing with the places in the neighbourhood of London reached by aircraft, or the course supposed to be taken by them, or any statement or diagram which might indicate the ground or route covered by them.

3rd June

Walter: Bert got this clipping from the Daily Mirror in the post – this year the races at Epsom was run by wounded soldiers instead of horses!

THE EPSOM SUMMER MEETING, 1915: THE ONLY "DERBY" AND "OAKS" THE FAMOUS DOWNS WILL SEE THIS YEAR.

(clockwise from top) Start of the "Oaks." Every runner had his left arm in splints, while the starter had lost his left leg

The "tip pump" tips a sure winner

Finish of the "Derby". "Happy" won in a canter

A section of the "crowd"

A "bookmaker" paying out

Carrying in a winner

| Ed: | What a sight! Mind you, I probably would have had better luck backing one of them than the lousy runners I've had lately. Get yourself a dodgy arm, Walt, and I'll put a shilling on you to win the National next year. |

5th June

| Walter: | How you getting on, Rose? It's a bit quieter here now. Moved to Verquin – doing route marches and more training. They get us doing fatigues too, which is a bit rich when we're supposed to be resting… had a few new recruits to make up the numbers after we lost so many though – they don't know what they're doing half of them, not like us veterans. Still waiting for Fred to get back from the M.O. |

| Rose: | Hello Walt. Hope Fred's alright – I'm so sorry you boys have had such a rotten time of it. I'm busy as ever… we're near Festubert, so if I had a motor and a proper day off it wouldn't take me long to come and see you! We're so near the action now that when the fighting's heavy we can't sleep – not just because of the extra wounded but because of the noise! I lie in bed just listening to the casualties racking up… had some very bad times lately with fellows dying on me, 24 in a fortnight. Glad you're getting a bit of a rest though – make the most of it. |

| Walter: | Thanks, Rosie. Sorry you've had a rough time. Did you hear back from your Scottish fellow with the amputation? |

| Rose: | Yes I did! His name's Jamie. We write to each other often now and he's getting on well with his recovery. I'll let you know when I get his next letter – he said he'd tell me about his rehabilitation treatment. |

8th June

| Walter: | 'Bathing parades' by the lake at Les Brebis today. In the army you can't be shy about getting your kit off in front of everyone! Most of the lads don't mind it, and you can bet our mate Duncan will be strutting about as usual… but poor Bert always looks like he'd rather the ground swallowed him up! At least the weather's hot, and we could all do with getting clean. Shame Fred's away – he'd love getting to lark about in the lake… I feel bad for him missing it, especially on his birthday. |

June 1915

Mabel:	Well, ain't you all handsome! I do miss our boys…
Lily:	Calm yourself, Mabel!

9th June

Rose:	Here's some news – I saw dear old Fred today! We had a visit to the convalescent hospital near GHQ (St Omer). The nurse who showed us round said it used to be a jute factory, but now it's all full of stretcher beds and men go there who've got ill from the trenches. She said you'd be surprised what getting clean, shaved and louse-free can do for them. They give them hot meals and disinfect their clothes too, and they've got an entertainment room with a piano in! Anyway, I didn't realise it was Fred at first, he looked so drawn, but I spotted the name on his bed. He was asleep, and looking the picture of peace, so I didn't disturb him – the nurse said he'd spent a few days in a shell hole, poor chap. But she reckoned he'd be fit enough to come back to you tomorrow, Walt. Ain't that good news? The men only stay here about a week – sometimes 10 days if they're really bad.

10th June

Lily:	Happy birthday sweetheart! Hope you get a quiet day and that my card arrives – I never know with you moving about so much.
Mary:	Happy birthday Walter! 20 years old already… have a good day, love. Keep safe.
Ed:	Happy birthday, little brother.
Rose:	Have a good birthday Walt! See if the others will let you have some extra rum.
Walter:	Thanks everyone for the birthday wishes, and for the parcels! I shared all the food out with the others… you should see the excitement when there's a birthday. It ain't a bad day out here neither – nice weather and we're not back in the line until tomorrow.

13th June

Walter:	Well, it's baking hot out here and we've taken over a section of the line from the 24th battalion. You've come back just in time for it to all get going again Fred! Sounds like you had a cushy time of it up at St Omer though… I wouldn't mind a hot bath and a nice nurse to look after me…
Fred:	I wouldn't have stayed long, Walt… it was nice and all but I wanted to get back to you lot. It's a strange thing – I spent days in that shell hole with no one but a dead fellow for company and then the moment I got meself together enough to crawl back I was whisked off to who knows where and it was all clean sheets and smiles and hot food… they said I looked so rotten I had to go, no arguments. I was lucky – plenty other wounded men don't get that luxury, eh? I kept dreaming I was back in that shell hole the first few days though. Sorry I missed your sister visiting.

Mabel: So glad you're alright Fred! It's baking here in London too – everyone's been out in the parks.

Fred: Hi Mabel. Thanks. What a picture... it seems a million miles away.

Fulham Park pond was popular with the children because of its excellent paddling facilities.

15th June

Walter: Writing from the trench. It's quite dark now and most of the platoon is trying to get some sleep, apart from the sentries of course. Just a few flashes from further down the line. I've had me promotion to Section Corporal approved – our Platoon Commander, Lt Summers, found me a few days ago and told me I'm now officially Cpl Dart's replacement. Had to draw stripes from the CQMS and sew them on. First test came pretty soon afterwards – got caught in a terrific bombardment earlier yesterday. Not much we could do though – just keep down and hope for the best. Thought they was going to attack afterwards but they didn't come. Waste of their shells – no serious casualties. There's a rumour we're going to have another go at them soon... can't say more yet.

Lily: Congratulations on your promotion, sweetheart. I'm not sure whether to be happy or worried for you as I expect it puts you in more danger, doesn't it? I do fret about you. And it's funny to think of you out there in the dark and me all tucked up in Battersea. We must seem very far away to you. Thank goodness you're still safe. How's Fred doing?

Walter: Hello Lil! It does seem strange to think of you lot back home – almost like a dream from years ago. I miss you. You mustn't worry about me though, I'm doing alright. Fred's cheering up a bit, but he's still a skinny rake and his old stiff arm has started playing him up again. He'll be fine – just needs a chance to get his confidence back. How are things in London now – no more Zepps?

Lily: No, no more Zepps. And the rioting's quietened down. Some days it just feels like normal again, except all our boys are gone and the food's so expensive. I miss you too. Look after yourself won't you, sweetheart? Goodnight!

The story of Walter Carter continues . . .

www.facebook.com/WW1SoldiersTale

www.twitter.com/WW1SoldiersTale

www.WW1SoldiersTale.co.uk/blog

ACKNOWLEDGEMENTS

First and foremost, massive thanks must go to Nikky Pye who has meticulously researched the whole of WWI, both from a military and a domestic viewpoint. She has beautifully written the posts accurately capturing not just the seemingly unending horrors of trench warfare but also the language of the time.

Huge thanks also to Diz Majores and Rachel Dixon. Diz first came up with the fascinating idea of telling a tale of a WWI soldier using social media and, with Rachel, has proofed all of the copy and made very sensible and creative suggestions as well as being responsible for posting in real time on Facebook, Twitter and the blog thereby building our considerable following. Key to the success of the project is to ensure that all posts are both historically accurate and authentic and we are very grateful to Derrick Harwood and Leslie McDonnell for checking all the copy and, using their vast and detailed knowledge of the War, providing invaluable advice.

We would like to thank Hugh Purcell of The Reserve Forces' and Cadets' Association for Greater London and Paul McCue of Wandsworth Council whose support from the very early days has been constant and positive. Also, David Cameron MP and Ed Vaizey MP, both of whom have given their personal support.

Finally, we would like to thank those organisations and individuals who have provided funding to date, to enable us to carry on with the project, which from the start has been on a non-profit making basis. These include:

Arms and Armour Heritage Trust

Brigadier (Ret'd) Paul Orchard-Lisle

David Noble for Living History

Department of Communities and Local Government

The Reserve Forces' and Cadets' Association for Greater London

The Royal Society of St George

The Worshipful Company of Barbers

The Worshipful Company of Coopers

The Worshipful Company of Information Technologists

Wandsworth Council

Image Credits

We would like to thank all those people and organisations that have assisted us in tracking down images, and granting permission to reproduce them. We have made every effort to give full and proper credits.

1914

16 March:	postcardsthenandnow.blogspot.com
27 March:	John Slusar at www.greyhoundderby.co.uk
3 April:	© TfL from the London Transport Museum collection
7 April:	www.recipespastandpresent.org.uk
11 April:	www.photodetective.co.uk
16 April:	© MirrorPix
23 April:	© MirrorPix
25 April:	© Illustrated London News Ltd/Mary Evans
8 May:	Express Newspapers/N&S Syndication
22 May:	© IWM (Q 81486)
28 May:	John Sulsar at www.greyhoundderby.co.uk
30 May:	Library and Archives Canada / PA-116389
9 June:	© Museum of London
15 June:	Daily Mirror
17 June:	© MirrorPix
25 June:	Image © The British Library Board. All rights reserved, reproduced with kind permission of The British Newspaper Archive, www.britishnewspaperarchive.co.uk
27 June:	© Victoria and Albert Museum, London
29 June:	Wiki Commons Europeana 1914-1918 collection
1 July:	Daily Mirror
2 July:	Wiki Commons Thetford, Owen (1994) British Naval Aircraft since 1912, London: Putnam, pp. p. 80
3 July:	Wiki Commons German submarine U9 (1914)
5 July:	Wiki Commons Library of the London School of Economics and Political Science
8 July:	www.disused-stations.org.uk
10 July:	Wiki Commons Postcard, c. 1911
11 July:	Wiki Commons The Suffragette by Sylvia Pankhurst. New York: Source Book Press, 1970. First published by Sturgis & Walton Company (New York), 1911. Facing p. 433
13 July:	Daily Mirror

14 July:	© Royal Armouries
15 July:	Daily Mirror
16 July:	Daily Mirror
18 July:	Wiki Commons http://www.johndclare.net/causes_WWI4.htm
21 July:	© The Board of Trinity College
28 July:	Wiki Commons The World's Work, 1919
29 July:	© D.C.Thomson & Co. Ltd. Image created courtesy of The British Library Board, reproduced with kind permission of The British Newspaper Archive www.britishnewspaperarchive.co.uk
2 August:	© Museum of London
3 August:	Daily Mirror
5 August:	© IWM (Q 81832)
5 August:	© www.chards.co.uk Permission has been gained for use of this photograph. Copyright remains with Chard (1964) Ltd
6 August:	© Royal Armouries
11 August:	With thanks to Linda Corbett from Ashton Pals, www.ashtonpals.webs.com
14 August:	© Museum of London
15 August:	© IWM (Q 51472)
24 August:	Wiki Commons Underwood & Underwood. (US War Dept.)
3 September:	Wiki Commons Bain News Service
7 September:	© Everett Collection Historical/Alamy Stock Photo
8 September:	© Royal Armouries
15 September:	© MirrorPix
15 September:	© MirrorPix
17 September:	© IWM (Q 57380)
17 September:	© Surrey History Centre
19 September:	© MirrorPix
21 September:	© Surrey History Centre
1 October:	State Library of South Australia [B 57607]
6 October:	Wiki Commons Men of Mark, Photographed from life by Lock and Whitfield, with brief biographical notices by Thompson Cooper
10 October:	Thanks to Jack Clegg
11 October:	Bibliothèque Nationale de France, Public Domain
18 October:	www.qcmilitaria.com
21 October:	Express Newspapers/N&S Syndication
29 October:	© IWM (EQU 56)

1 November:	The White Feather: A Sketch of English Recruiting by Arnold Bennett, Collier's Weekly 1914
10 November:	Daily Mirror
16 November:	Daily Mirror
17 November:	British Red Cross archives
28 November:	Newspapers/N&S Syndication
1 December:	Express Newspapers/N&S Syndication
3 December:	Express Newspapers/N&S Syndication
5 December:	www.worldwar1postcards.com
9 December:	© National Maritime Museum, Greenwich, London
10 December:	Express Newspapers/N&S Syndication
14 December:	www.garenewing.co.uk, Photograph courtesy Garen Ewing
21 December:	© Mary Evans Picture Library/Alamy Stock Photo
23 December:	Wiki Commons The Sketch, 1895
24 December:	© IWM (Q 71937)
27 December:	© Harold Robson/IWM (Q 50719)
29 December:	Express Newspapers/N&S Syndication
31 December:	Express Newspapers/N&S Syndication

1915

1 January:	www.worldwar1postcards.com
2 January:	Lyme Regis Philpot Museum
7 January:	Daily Mirror
8 January:	Daily Mirror
9 January:	Express Newspapers/N&S Syndication
15 January:	Express Newspapers/N&S Syndication
20 January:	© IWM (Q 53599)
25 January:	Daily Mirror
4 February:	Daily Mirror
5 February:	Express Newspapers/N&S Syndication
11 February:	Daily Mirror
12 February:	Express Newspapers/N&S Syndication
15 February:	Daily Mirror
18 February:	Daily Mirror
22 February:	Daily Mirror
26 February:	Daily Mirror

2 March:	Wiki Commons Published in Vanity Fair, 17 March 1910
17 March:	www.worldwar1postcards.com
20 March:	From How I Filmed the War by Geoffrey H. Malins, Project Gutenberg license
23 March:	Express Newspapers/N&S Syndication
31 March:	Express Newspapers/N&S Syndication
6 April:	Express Newspapers/N&S Syndication
9 April:	IWM (Q 67407)
12 April:	Express Newspapers/N&S Syndication
23 April:	Wiki Commons, originally from Collier's New Photographic History of the World's War (New York, 1918)
25 April:	Express Newspapers/N&S Syndication
28 April:	Burton, H M. The Defence Department of the Commonwealth. Courtesy of www.awm.gov.au
1 May:	Express Newspapers/N&S Syndication
4 May:	Daily Mirror
6 May:	Express Newspapers/N&S Syndication
8 May:	Express Newspapers/N&S Syndication
13 May:	Daily Mirror
14 May:	Daily Mirror
14 May:	www.worldwar1postcards.com
16 May:	Daily Mirror
22 May:	Express Newspapers/N&S Syndication
24 May:	Reproduced by permission of the Trustees of the former DLI and Durham County Record Office. © Durham County Record Office D/DLI/2/6/10 (317)
27 May:	Thanks to www.flickr.com/photos/16118167@N04/
28 May:	Express Newspapers/N&S Syndication
1 June:	Express Newspapers/N&S Syndication
3 June:	Daily Mirror
8 June:	Reproduced by permission of the National Library of Scotland
13 June:	Daily Mirror